# ABERDEEN'S UNION TERRACE GARDENS

Union Terrace Gardens from the air in 1948. It seems amazing that the Gardens should have survived in such a situation for this length of time.

# ABERDEEN'S UNION TERRACE GARDENS

WAR AND PEACE IN THE DENBURN VALLEY

## DIANE MORGAN
WITH AN ADDITIONAL CHAPTER BY MIKE SHEPHERD

BLACK & WHITE PUBLISHING

First published 2015
by Black & White Publishing Ltd
29 Ocean Drive, Edinburgh EH6 6JL

1 3 5 7 9 10 8 6 4 2    15 16 17 18

ISBN: 978 1 84502 494 9

Copyright © Diane Morgan 2015
Chapter 13 copyright © Michael Shepherd 2015

The right of Diane Morgan and Michael Shepherd to be identified as the authors of this work has been asserted by them in accordance with the Copyright, Designs and Patents Act 1988.

All rights reserved. No part of this publication may be reproduced, stored in a retrieval system, or transmitted in any form, or by any means, electronic, mechanical, photocopying, recording or otherwise, without permission in writing from the publisher.

The publisher has made every reasonable effort to contact copyright holders of images in this book. Any errors are inadvertent and anyone who, for any reason, has not been contacted is invited to write to the publisher so that a full acknowledgment can be made in subsequent editions of this work.

A CIP catalogue record for this book is available from the British Library.

Typeset by Creative Link, North Berwick
Printed and bound by Gutenberg Press, Malta

For all Friends of Union Terrace Gardens

I am native here

*Hamlet*, Act 1, Scene 4

# CONTENTS

Acknowledgements (viii)

Preface (xi)

**Chapter One**
Early Days Around the Denburn Valley 1

**Chapter Two**
The Great Bleachery 17

**Chapter Three**
From the Corbie Heugh to Union Terrace Gardens 39

**Chapter Four**
James Forbes Beattie: The Forgotten Designer
of Union Terrace Gardens 55

**Chapter Five**
High Society in Union Terrace 65

**Chapter Six**
Viaducts, Balustrades and Other Things 81

**Chapter Seven**
The Very Place for Statues 99

**Chapter Eight**
John Gray 1811–1891: The Ideal Benefactor                    119

**Chapter Nine**
Disruption in the Denburn Valley                              125

**Chapter Ten**
Turrets, Towers, Spires, Domes, Diesels and Dual Carriageway  145

**Chapter Eleven**
The Gardens, Mostly in the Twentieth Century                  161

**Chapter Twelve**
'The Best Laid Schemes of Mice and Men . . .'                 177

**Chapter Thirteen**
The Battle for Union Terrace Gardens: Mike Shepherd Reports   187

**Chapter Fourteen**
Some Random Thoughts                                          207

**Chapter Fifteen**
In Retrospect                                                 219

**Bibliography**                                              229

**Index**                                                     233

# ACKNOWLEDGEMENTS

My special thanks go to Irene Bryce who has provided invaluable help, support and brilliant scans, all of which are much appreciated. Keith Jones gave advice about the railways, Norman Marr about the dual carriageway piles and Dr Andrew Cameron about the likes and dislikes of the Dutch Elm Beetle. Mrs Heather Stoddart wrote to reveal that it was her grandfather William Dyack, Deputy Burgh Surveyor, who made the suggestion that the Union Terrace balustrades should run from the Denburn Viaduct to Union Bridge, and supervised their erection. That was a great talking point, and it set a trend. I had hoped to report on the opening of the 'Caley Tunnel' linking the Caledonian Hotel – its entrance is in the basement – and Union Terrace Gardens, emerging in the vicinity of Robert Burns' statue, but that idea has been shelved for the time being. Thanks to Ian Flett of the Maintenance Department for keeping me advised. Thanks too to Midge and Charles Miller, and to Catherine Taylor and John Souter for advice in days gone by.

Kate Sutherland took the excellent modern photographs of the Wallace Statue in Rosemount Viaduct and we were amazed to see how active Sir William seemed, moving around, in command of the whole area. J A Sutherland drew the artist's impressions and illustrations on pages 151, 174 and 176. We are especially indebted for his beautiful line drawing of the Union Terrace Bandstand at the end of the book.

Roddy Millar has kindly made available superb and distinctive photographs for the front cover, and of the Gardens and whole area, including those on pages 91, 93, 94, 148, 150 and 158. They deserve a book of their own. The wonderful group shot in Chapter 11 is by courtesy of Roddy and in Chapter 10 the three vintage railway images are courtesy of Great North of Scotland Railway Association, while the modern image is by

Roddy. Mike Shepherd has provided an excellent selection of his own work, not only of the Gardens, but of the 'Priory', (complete with bartizans), the UTG light iron bridge in the Duthie Park and, a superb shot of Britannia trying to break the Sword of War beside Edward VII's statue. Below them, the still famous Gents' was photographed by Alex Guyan. Other illustrative material is from the author's collection.

The panoramic image of Union Terrace was supplied by Alex Mitchell, the Rose Walk by Clifford Milne and Bertie the Blogger by his amanuensis, Dr Gail Reikie.

The confrontation between sheep and coach in the Denburn, and Wallace in Winter (1899) are by courtesy of Neil Blair and Aberdeen Camera Club. The unusual photograph of Wallace hailing the Triple Kirks in springtime, standing beside the Rosemount Viaduct 'triangle' filled with bedding plants is from The Free West by J Ogilvie Skea, (AUP, 1963).

I have pleasure in acknowledging permission to reproduce copyright material kindly provided by the following institutions.

RCAHMS – for the Frontispiece
Aberdeen Library and Information Services for p32, p60, p75, p134, p140, p141 and p146.
Aberdeen Journals Ltd for p172.
The banknote on p137 featuring Mary Slessor is by kind consent of the Clydesdale Bank.

# PREFACE

The architect Alexander Marshall Mackenzie argued passionately 'that the Denburn Valley is the only natural feature in Aberdeen. It is important that it should be kept as an open space with its present appearance.'

> William Robbie, *Aberdeen: Its Traditions and History* (1893)

The complete story of Union Terrace Gardens in the heart of Aberdeen has never been written. Before the next *folie de grandeur* comes along, as come it will, this book will attempt to chart the history of the present Gardens and the Denburn Valley from the late seventeenth century to the second decade of the twenty-first when the Gardens came close to extinction. (Correction: the next *folie de grandeur* has come along as I write, or as I should correctly call it: the draft Aberdeen City Centre Master Plan, which was announced on 10 March. Among other things, a bridge is planned, linking the Gardens and Belmont Street, but this is far in the future).

How does Union Terrace Gardens – that name is the most recent of several – relate to the Denburn Valley, for the two are often spoken of together? Union Terrace Gardens occupies the west side of the Valley, which runs almost but not quite between Woolmanhill and the Green. From the seventeenth century, perhaps earlier, until the latter part of the nineteenth, that steep bank – Union Terrace sits above it – was known as the Corbie Heugh, the crow cliff, usually mentioned in conjunction with 'the rig of land below,' at the bottom of the Valley. The 'rig' extended across to the Denburn, which used to flow in open cut near the east side. The burn has long been converted and flows mainly if not entirely under the railway line. Thus the old Corbie Heugh, and the land below as far as the railway wall form Union Terrace Gardens, and occupy the greater part of the Denburn Valley.

The former Triple Kirks mark the northern end of the Denburn Valley's easterly cliff, which, as Parson Gordon's map of 1661 indicates, was, if anything, even steeper than the Corbie Heugh. It too headed towards the Green but was more severely eroded by 'the works of man' than the Heugh: by the sloping rear gardens of the eighteenth-century houses of Belmont Street, by the development of Mutton Brae, of the Triple Kirks of 1843-1844, the Denburn Valley Junction Railway of 1867 and the Rosemount Viaduct of 1883-1886. They all took their toll. The Denburn Valley, in fact, has lost one of its sides.

How did the present Union Terrace Gardens and their immediate environs continue to survive long after the area around was enfolded by the city? Initially the place had something to offer fulfilling several roles in the agricultural, the industrial, and eventually, the recreational life of the city. The flat land, incidentally, at the bottom of the Valley was known during its industrial era as the Great Bleachery. At the end of this era, the future Gardens were in grave danger of being swamped with houses. Fortunately a champion emerged, the architect James Matthews. Without his drive and perseverance they would have vanished. The story of how the Gardens of today emerged under his guidance and determination is one of the main themes of this volume.

Part of the area's richness lies in the Gardens' magnificent architectural hinterland. Matthews' pupil, and later his partner, the great A Marshall Mackenzie, working in Union Terrace, played a major role at the north end there. One of Matthews & Mackenzie's clients, John Gray, was responsible not only for funding the School of Art that bears his name, but for the arched entrance to Robert Gordon's College, and the Public Library and St Mark's Kirk in Rosemount Viaduct as well. In the Viaduct in the late sun of an early spring afternoon the 'amazing parade' (as John Betjeman described it) of domes, towers, turrets, spires and bartizans, stretching from the Library to the Academy, all magically aglow, is one of the most amazing sights that Aberdeen has to offer.

The 'war' of 2008–2012 began with a few folk determined not to lose the Gardens ranged against a phalanx of wealth, business interests and formidable publicity. The few folk became the Friends of Union Terrace

# PREFACE

Gardens, have grown greatly in number and have shown the city how to conduct a well-informed and intelligent public protest. Mike Shepherd, the first Chairman, excelled in quiet leadership, tenacity and the ability to hold firm under fire. We are fortunate in having a crucial chapter from him.

A final point. Parks and landscaped gardens can now be listed in the same way as buildings and monuments. Historic Scotland who are responsible for listing, have spoken highly of the Gardens, of their role in the city centre, and the unique quality of their architectural hinterland. I would say to them that the time for listing a city centre park as important as Union Terrace Gardens is long overdue.

Diane Morgan

Chapter One

# EARLY DAYS AROUND THE DENBURN VALLEY

The formidable nature of both the Denburn Valley – roughly some 600 yards long – and the burn itself, snaking through it like some malignant sea serpent without head or tail, is clearly shown in the illustration overleaf. This is a detail from the earliest map of the burgh. Published in 1661 it was the work of James Gordon, Parson of Rothiemay in Banffshire, historian, draughtsman and cartographer *par excellence*. Parson Gordon's skills were inherited from his father, Robert Gordon of Straloch, cartographer to Charles I, who with the king's encouragement, ensured that 'Scotland was one of the best mapped countries in the world.'

The source of the Denburn is at Kingswells about six miles west of Aberdeen. The burn provided water-power for the famous Mill of Maidencraig, then flowed on through the ravine at Woodend and further downstream through the gorge of Rubislaw Den, which was possibly even more spectacular than the Denburn Valley though different in character. Rubislaw Den was largely inaccessible until the building of the Skene Turnpike, or at least the Queen's Road section of it. Thereafter 'the Den' became home to Aberdeen's wealthiest.

On reaching Aberdeen, the Denburn skirted the home stretch of the Skene Turnpike, now the lower end of Skene Street, and flowed under Collie's Brig at its foot. That took it to the Woolmanhill, once a market where sheep were sold, and 'a little green swelling hill' in Gordon's time. This was the gateway to the Denburn Valley at its north end as the left side of the map shows – an easy walk from the centre of the burgh and a popular place for leisure and recreation. The valley is not named specifically but the Corby Heugh (as Parson Gordon spells 'Corbie') – the future Union Terrace Gardens – and the serpentine Denn Burn are clearly noted. The Playe Greene ('playe' as in acting) is top left in the detail from Gordon's Plan.

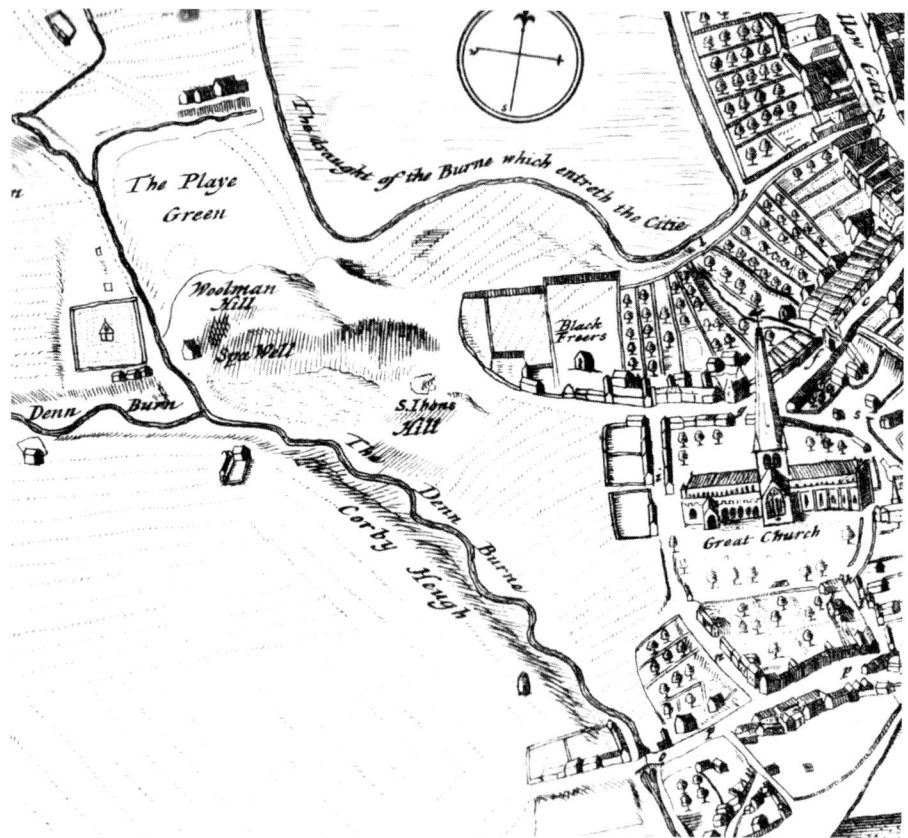

*The Denburn Valley occupies the eastern half of this plan with the Denburn snaking its way along the bottom, east of the wooded slope of the 'Corby Heugh' - the future Union Terrace Gardens, The pepper pot-shaped Doocot is near the lower end with the Doocot Croft below. This was where General Cope's army was encamped in 1745. Note the little twin-arched Bow Brig, built by Andrew Jamesone, to the right of the croft. The Green, marked 'P' is extreme right, and above it, the Great Church of St Nicholas dominates the central area. The upper quarter of the plan shows the 'leisure and recreation' area at the gateway to the Denburn Valley with the 'Playe Greene', 'Spa Well' etc. To the right is the Blackfriars Monastery, ruinous since the Reformation of 1560. Robert Gordon's College – he was the nephew of Parson Gordon – was built on this site. Detail from Parson Gordon's Plan of 1661.*

Non-paying spectators could watch *al fresco* performances from a vantage point on the Woolmanhill, just as their descendants would stand on the Broad Hill to watch the Dons playing at Pittodrie.

Below the Woolmanhill was the Spa Well, sitting in its little well house. It was famed far and wide for its medicinal properties, and the hospitals at Woolmanhill were built in its vicinity. It included among its satisfied clientele, the famed portrait painter George Jamesone (1590–1644), who lived nearby in the handsome family home in Schoolhill. George Jamesone was cured of 'the calculus' or stone in the bladder by drinking the Well's water. In gratitude, Jamesone had a small, one might even say petite, pleasure ground – the Four Neukit Garden – Aberdeen's first public park, laid out for the enjoyment of local people, just north of the future Union Terrace Gardens. Though unnamed it can be easily identified on the map by its four neuks or corners, and the little summerhouse in the centre. Parson Gordon describes Jamesone, who would have known the Denburn Valley well, as 'an ingenious paynter who did sett up therein ane timber hous paynted all over with his own hand.' Jamesone wasn't just Scotland's earliest portrait painter: he could turn his hand to house painting if required.

Before Jamesone created the Four Neukit Garden, the same terrain had an earlier life as a 'Playe Field', an open-air theatre, before it was superseded by the larger 'Playe Green' to the north. It was on the Playe Field that 'a company of comedians' (actors) from the Royal Globe Theatre in London entertained the locals for a three-weeks season in October 1601. They were fêted by the magistrates and their manager, Lawrence Fletcher, and the company were made Freemen of the City. King James VI, who enjoyed a good play, had organised the players' visit, first to Edinburgh then on to Aberdeen, with the consent of Queen Elizabeth of England with whom he maintained good relations. William Shakespeare was a member of the Royal Globe Company at this time, which leaves the teasing question – did Shakespeare come to Aberdeen? There is no positive proof, though in his book *City by the Grey North Sea: Aberdeen* (1966) the local historian Fenton Wyness has suggested that the landscape of the Mounth, which the actors would have crossed en route, could have inspired the 'blasted heath' scenes in *Macbeth*, which Shakespeare began to write in 1605. Had the celebrated playwright been here, he may well have taken a turn in the easily accessible Corbie Heugh, whose wooded cliff adjoined the Playe Field on the west side of the Valley.

We are lucky to have Parson Gordon's sketch of the Four Neukit Garden. He shows it sitting near the confluence of the Gilcomston Burn which flowed down from the north, with the Denburn from the west, both unpredictable and unruly streams, quite capable of swamping the Denburn Valley. A few years after the Parson completed his invaluable map, the Four Neukit Garden was devastated by a particularly fierce spate. The summerhouse was shattered, as was the wellhouse of the Spa Well. Earth and debris were thrown over the Woolmanhill and the healing spring waters vanished underground. In a few years time, fortunately, the spring re-emerged, and

*The Well of Spa, above, in what is said to be its original site, and below, several moves later, the restored wellhead in the Denburn car park. When planned demolitions take place in this area, the wellhead will be on the move again.*

was reunited with its patched-up wellhouse, the gable of which still survives though much restored. George Jamesone had settled in Edinburgh where his popularity as a portrait painter kept him extremely busy. He did return to Aberdeen from time to time, but never rebuilt the little 'timber hous'.

Returning to Gordon's Plan, the east side of the Denburn Valley, not yet eroded by the works of man, is shown rising steeply from the east side of the burn – the Denburnside. Where the ground levels out, the Great Church of St Nicholas, named in honour of the burgh's patron saint, is shown, a cathedral *manqué* if ever there was one. Its origins are speculatively twelfth century, and the original reason for siting it or its predecessor so far from what was then the budding settlement of Aberdeen has never been satisfactorily explained.

Parson Gordon's name of 'Great Church ' is a trifle out of date for 1661. With the establishment of Presbyterianism some years after the Reformation of 1560 the 'Great Church' still retained its pre-Reformation layout but the name had changed. The nave, the people's area to the west, became the Auld, the Toun or West Kirk, while the choir to the east, sacred to the clergy, became the New or East Kirk, two churches for the price of one. It has the same pre-Reformation configuration to this day, though the buildings have changed. Of the transepts between the churches, the one on the south side, shown below the spire on Gordon's map, became Drum's Aisle, a great treasure of the kirk. Its opposite number to the north (not visible on the map), Collison's Aisle, was endowed by the 'ambesowus and prood' Provost John Collison. It is now home to St John's Chapel, a chapel for the oil industry in Aberdeen, with contemporary furnishings and cheerful stained glass.

The Westerkirkgate, (*gate*: Scots, road) unnamed on Gordon's map, runs along the west side of St Nicholas Kirk. It was and remains the west road to the kirk though for centuries now it has been called Back Wynd. To the left of the Great Church, a few dwellings sit in sizeable enclosures, sloping towards the Denburn. The town is expanding as far west as it can go before the eastern slope of the Valley intervenes, but there will still be room a hundred years hence to tuck Belmont Street in above the burn. The name is appropriate, for the views across the Valley would indeed have been and are

*Sheep on the Skene Turnpike probably en route for the Denburn Valley. They are passing the Old House of Rubislaw. No. 50 Queen's Road now stands on this site.*

*A 'standoff' near Woolmanhill as a flock of sheep is driven towards the Denburn Valley. Even if this incident was posed for the camera, it is more than likely to have reflected a real-life occurrence.*

*belle*, beautiful, and as for the *mont* – the street is perched along the top of a cliff. Stand in the car park at the rear of Black & Lizars at No. 38 Belmont Street today, or look down Patagonian Court and you'll get some idea of the original steepness of the East Bank.

The Denburn flowed not quite through the centre of the Valley, but nearer the east side. One access from the town, not in existence in Parson Gordon's time, was a path leading from the Westerkirkgate/Back Wynd down to the burn. Belmont Street cut across it in the 1770s but the path can still be traced today, as Gaelic Lane and Patagonian Court.

Access to the Valley from the country areas of the north and west had a long association with sheep, as local place names suggest. Woolmanhill could have been a market for selling sheep as opposed to fleeces and wool. The sale of the latter, in the weekly market in the Green, was seasonal, held only about half-a-dozen times a year around shearing time. In the 1690s, according to the First Statistical Account, there were over a thousand sheep in the parish of Skene, west of Aberdeen. They would have been herded to town by a drover, initially along the Old Skene Road, which ended at today's Skene Square – and so down to Woolmanhill and onto the northern end of Denburn Meadows, possibly the Valley's earliest and most pleasant name, with its ample grass and water. Around 1800 the Old Skene Road was superseded by the new

*A busy scene in Windmill Brae. The balustrades and obelisks of the Bow Brig, complete with lamps, can be made out at the foot of the Brae. Hadden's great woollen mill dominates the middle distance.*

*The turreted house of the artist George Jamesone in Schoolhill. It was built by his father, the mason Andrew Jamesone in 1586 and demolished, amid great protest in, 1886.*

## EARLY DAYS AROUND THE DENBURN VALLEY

Skene Turnpike, which arrived in Aberdeen via the future Queen's Road, Carden Place and Skene Street, ending then where it does today at the rear of His Majesty's Theatre. No theatre then of course and no Rosemount Viaduct. The sheep could simply be driven round into the Valley. Several illustrations of sheep and their shepherds in this area are extant. The mysteriously named Patagonian Court – Patagonian Close until the 1920s – could well have been inspired by Patagonia in Chile which developed a massive sheep trade during the nineteenth century. A returning sailor or merchant may have looked down the close one day when the Denburn Valley was packed with sheep and remarked 'It 'minds me o' Patagonia.'

A curious incident was reported in 1693 when the grass in the Denburn Meadows 'was eaten up and destroyed by flocks of sheep.' The rough pasturelands of Gilcomston to the north had been rented by a Mr Thomas Garden of Banchory for grazing his flocks. The 'moutons', having munched their way through the Gilcomston grass, sensed pastures new in the adjoining Denburn Valley. It was no distance at all to the short springy turf of St John's Hill which Parson Gordon shows just south east of the Woolmanhill. It received the same treatment as Gilcomston, and 'not a blade of grass was left standing there.' St John's Hill then vanishes from history, but I suspect that after this episode it was nicknamed Mutton Brae, which seems to have occupied the same place. The name stuck. When not required for corralling sheep at the time of the sales, the Valley was given over to common grazing.

At the foot of the Plan, the Bow Brig ('bow' being an arch) over the Denburn, was built where there was no great chasm to loup. The Brig, though small, was a notable landmark on the sole route into Aberdeen from the south, linking the Bridge of Dee, the Hardgate and its continuation, Windmill Brae, on the one side with the Green and Aberdeen proper on the other.

There were several Bow Brigs over the years but possibly the first to be built 'of stane and lyme' instead of wood was the work, in 1556, of Robert Lumsden, Master of the Bridge of Dee Work. A substantial structure was necessary to cope with the extra traffic generated by the Bridge of Dee, which was initiated by William Elphinstone, Bishop of Aberdeen and completed in 1527 by his worthiest successor, Gavin Dunbar, and still with us – the bridge,

# UNION TERRACE GARDENS

*The single arch Bow Brig, by James Jeans, with the curious obelisks on the parapet is glimpsed beyond the splendid arch of the recently built Union Bridge. In the foreground is the common bleach-green or bleachery which became the lowest level of Union Terrace Gardens. Left foreground is a little pack bridge over the Denburn, with another beyond the pegged-out garments and weavers' webs – the newly woven cloth from the loom. More webs are being laid on the bleachgreen. Glimpses of the gardens of Belmont Street, left and the Corbie Heugh and railing, right.*

that is, not Bishop Dunbar who, incidentally, mortified (endowed) rents from his Lands of Ardlair in the parish of Clatt for its upkeep. The Bridge of Dee Fund had been earlier initiated by Bishop Elphinstone and was also used to maintain the various Bow Brigs over the years, which inevitably were taking as much traffic as the Bridge of Dee.

Lumsden's bridge was the usual 'brig of twa bowis,' not a good idea, for when the Denburn was roaring down in one of its spates to what passed for the harbour estuary, debris would get trapped within the two narrow arches and flood not only the Valley but the Green as well. Nevertheless, the Town persisted with the 'twa bowis' design in 1586 and again in 1609 when the master mason was Andrew Jamesone, father of the painter George of Four Neukit fame, and builder of the splendid turreted Jamesone house in Schoolhill. It was demolished in 1886 as a traffic hazard to cries of outrage.

Travellers to Aberdeen from the south, whoever they were: kings, queens, lairds, soldiers, country folk, merchants, pedlars, tinkers, caterans, had to cross the Denburn by the Bow Brig. They would have had a spectacular view up the Denburn Valley, though at the Battle of Justice Mill on 13

September 1644, the Marquis of Montrose's 'wilde Irishes' would have been too focused on the prospect of sacking Aberdeen to notice. In peaceful times the Brig was a great gathering place for news and gossip. It was here that countrywomen delivered the shanks (stocking legs) they had knitted for the woollen merchants who provided them with the yarn. Old Baillie Hadden whose house was near the Bow Brig would come out to greet his knitters there. He did not live to see the completion of the great Hadden woollen mill, Alex Hadden & Sons, in Rennie's Wynd, whose great lum dominated the airspace above the Green for so long. But in its creation, his sons James and Gavin, both provosts of Aberdeen in their day, perpetuated his name. The country people also brought dairy produce for sale and that is how the popular Friday market at the Green developed, but these days, apart from the flowers, plants and vegetables, it is scarcely a shadow of its former self.

A particularly bad flood in November 1746 put an end to the Andrew Jamesone bridge which had endured nearly 140 years. It was replaced in 1747 by a single-span Bow Brig at last, the work of John Jeans, a local architect and master mason of repute. It was built in dressed granite and with a span 'of very neat workmanship'. The versatile Francis Douglas, traveller, writer, publisher, poet, farmer and baker of 'Abbot's Inch, near Paisley' visited Aberdeen in the summer of 1780, and noted it in his *Description of the East Coast of Scotland* as 'a handsome bridge of one arch thrown over a rivulet called the Denburn.' John Jeans is also credited for the house at No. 64 Broad Street, at that time one of the finest streets in Aberdeen where George Gordon, the future Lord Byron, and his mother had an apartment between 1791 and 1798. Its six long windows faced the busy street, the start of the only route north, so the small boy would have had much to look out on. That was part of a heterogeneous terrace which fronted the Marischal College of that era which had been completed by William Adam in the mid-eighteenth century. In those days the College was entered by a pend some yards north of the Byron dwelling.

It is the John Jeans' Bow Brig that we see in the distance in early illustrations of Union Bridge looking south. The Brig was superfluous by 1805 when Union Street was completed and Union Bridge was open for

*The Garden's arches housed several structures, one of which was thought to be the old Bow Brig. But which one?*

business, yet folk continued to use the old, difficult Hardgate, Windmill Brae, Bow Brig, and Green route into Aberdeen for years, because they were familiar places. The new entrance to the city via Holburn Street and Union Street beckoned, but the new buildings going up there, though impressive to behold, remained thinly spread. This new scenario was formidable rather than friendly.

In 1850 the Police Commissioners ordered the polluted lower reaches of the Denburn which flowed under the Bow Brig to be covered in, rendering it totally superfluous. For some months the Brig straddled dry land and might have been left as a curiosity were it not for the fact that it attracted loafers and persons of ill repute. It was demolished in 1851, though each stone was numbered, in the hope of resurrection. 'The Bridge, having stood for one hundred and four years, may now be seen lying in a disjointed mass, at the north-west corner of Union Bridge, biding its time,' so wrote James Rettie, jeweller and local historian, in 1868 in *Aberdeen 150 Years Ago*.

There is some confusion about the ultimate fate of the Bow Brig. Its components were said to have been used in the construction of the Union Terrace Garden's grotto at a later date. Alternatively it was said to have been taken to the rear of one of the arches of Union Terrace Gardens and fitted up there, or perhaps used as a template for the famous arcade of granite arches in the Gardens. Its true identity is now a mystery. The Bow Brig was replaced by a graceful footbridge when the railway was built in 1865–1867 and later, about 1919, by the rough and ready wooden 'Puffin' Briggie'. Local lads, on the approach of a train would lay their caps on the deck and see them wafted aloft by steam from steam engines when they passed under the bridge. The intrepid reader can still enter the town via the Windmill Brae and the Green route, an ancient right of way, though not now a very satisfactory one. Dreary and sometimes dangerous, Windmill Brae is a far cry from the jolly print on page 7 but screw your courage to the sticking place, walk to the foot of it and climb the stairs of the car park there. About halfway across on the central walkway which replaces the old Bow Brigs and the footbridges, you can crouch down to get the view of Union Bridge similar to the one that travellers would have had after 1805 – but not identical, for a steel corset was fixed onto the Bridge in 1907 to support its widening. You can then continue down the stairs at the other end of the walkway and so to the Green.

We can now complete our circular tour of the Denburn Valley and follow Parson Gordon to the famous west side of the Valley where the forerunners of Union Terrace Gardens, Doocot Brae (a 'doo' being Scots for a dove or pigeon) and the adjoining Corbie Heugh await. This area was even more accessible from the south end than from the north. A short track just east of the Bow Brig took one up to the Doocot Brae and the Doocot Croft – sometimes called the Templar Croft, for this land was once owned by the Templar Knights (today you'll find the Monkey House bar on this site, at the start of Union Terrace). A little further north stood the Doocot, or Dove Cott, itself. In view of the prominence which Parson Gordon gives it (it sits

*Modern corbies in the trees of Corbie Heugh, at the Union Street end of Union Terrace Gardens. Note the French influence, corbie from* corbeau, *a crow, not to mention* mouton, *as in Mutton Brae, a sheep.*

some distance south of 'Corby Heugh' on the Plan), it must have been of substantial construction and a well-known landmark. It provided a roosting place for great flocks of pigeons, and they in turn provided pigeon pie for citizens in times when food was scarce. A second track divided the arable Doocot Croft lands from the adjoining Corbie Heugh which was wooded and where visitors on market days could tether their ponies. They could then make their way downwards to the lowest level of the Valley where another path would take them out onto the Bow Brig and so into Aberdeen. For those not hurrying into town, the wooded slopes of the Corbie Heugh (Parson Gordon spells it Corby) offered a pleasant walk, stretching as far north as Woolmanhill and the Playe Green in those pre-Rosemount Viaduct days, or east across to the Denburn, over the very ground which became Union Terrace Gardens.

Heugh is a North-east word meaning a precipice, crag, cliff or steep hill, or a steep-sided glen or ravine, thus the whole of the Denburn Valley can be regarded as a heugh. Corbie Heugh on the west side of the Valley was the home of the corbies or crows, certainly established there by the seventeenth century, and doubtless since the time there were trees to inhabit. Some later cartographers and commentators, perhaps misreading Gordon's writing or copying later writers, have called it Corbie Haugh but that is not correct, in fact the meaning is quite the reverse. A haugh is low-lying ground. Heughs are scattered around the rocky North-east and a similar place name is Fowlsheugh, the seabird colony on the cliffs south of Stonehaven.

During the Rising of 1745, General Sir John Cope and his army of over 2,000 government redcoats, having missed the Jacobite army at Inverness, marched into Aberdeen on 10 September 1745 and encamped on the Doocot Brae 'amidst the ripe standing corn' in spite of remonstrance, and spilled into the Corbie Heugh. While awaiting the arrival of the transports, the ships that would take his army south, Cope took the opportunity to carry out a quick reconnaissance of the town's fortifications. He then sent for Provost Morison and the magistrates and told them that he had observed cannon at the fort on the harbour mouth – the Blockhouse – and had also been advised that the town possessed a considerable number of small arms. 'Would they,' Cope asked, 'incline to send them along with the transports to prevent their falling into any enemy's hands?' The magistrates were not too unhappy to give up the cannon, since they had been bought solely for defence of the harbour and could not be used against a land force, or so it was thought. But there was a consensus against handing over small arms. The following day the magistrates met again with the General who, sensing their reluctance, advised that if they retained the small arms, and if these arms 'be afterwards be seized upon by ane enemy, the town would lay themselves obnoxious to the government and made answerable for such conduct.' Thus threatened, the magistrates caved in and gave up the small arms. And so Cope sailed south to confront the Jacobites, with 'six fine twelve-pounders dismantled from the Blockhouse and 250 stand of muskets and ammunition,' and left Aberdeen defenceless. His army had also stripped the burgh of food and provender, had trampled down the crops ripening around the Doocot Croft and damaged the growing wood of the Corbie Heugh.

Cope and his redcoats did not fare well at the ensuing Battle of Prestonpans on 21 September, caught on the hop in one of the most famous episodes of the Forty-Five and prompting the Jacobite song 'Hey, Johnnie Cope are ye waukin yet?' Cope was not heard much of after that.

CHAPTER TWO

# THE GREAT BLEACHERY

The unpleasant affair with Sir John Cope was by no means the only nuisance in the Aberdeen area created by combatants involved in the Jacobite Rising of 1745. Though Cope and his forces departed on 15 September, other uninvited guests arrived. The Jacobites marched into town ten days later and at the Market Cross in the Castlegate proclaimed the Old Pretender, king – as James VIII. He was father of the Jacobite leader, Charles Edward Stuart – Bonnie Prince Charlie, the Young Pretender. Provost Morison who had been taken to the Cross under duress 'with some broadswords over my head' refused to drink a toast of loyalty to the Prince and as he put it rather mildly afterwards 'I had a glass of wine spilt down my breast.' The Jacobites occupied the city and busied themselves attempting to impose taxes. They remained in control until word reached them of the approach of King George II's second son, the Duke of Cumberland, at the head of a Government army. The Jacobites quickly marched off north.

The Duke of Cumberland rode over the Bow Brig on 27 February 1746 and continued on through the Green, the Westerkirkgate and the Upperkirkgate to Marischal College (a predecessor of the present splendid pile) where the rooms originally provided for him were rejected as too damp. He lodged instead for some months across the road in the Guestrow at Sir George Skene's Mansion before setting out to put paid to the Jacobite cause. Controversy continues as to his behaviour during his stay in Aberdeen with some arguing that he was quite the model lodger, others the reverse. He seems to have been popular with the magistrates who made him a Freeman of the City. During its later days as a common lodging house, Sir George Skene's Mansion was known as Cumberland House in recollection of its notorious guest. Now it is called Provost Skene's House, and will re-open

# UNION TERRACE GARDENS

'Cumberland House', now Provost Skene's House.

'Fort Cumberland' – the Auld Hoose at Robert Gordon's College.

to the public when the latest building works around it allow. It is a great survivor even though its career has been chequered.

Cumberland had considerable forces in the city – 3,900 redcoats plus 5,000 Hanoverian auxiliaries some of whom were encamped in the public gardens in front of Robert Gordon's Hospital, these days within the curtilage of the college. It had been completed in 1731 but was not yet occupied. The cavalry stabled their horses in nearby St Nicholas Kirkyard, and stored their provender within the two kirks there. The Quaker Meeting House in the Guestrow was transformed into a Temple of Mammon, as it were, and was requisitioned for use as a mint, presumably to pay troops and suppliers.

The magistrates had dreaded Cumberland's eventual departure, fearing the city would be left open to attack from the Highlanders of Strathdon and Glenlivet, lurking in the hinterland and led by the aged but charismatic Gordon of Glenbucket, a perfervid Jacobite. But Cumberland allayed their fears by converting Gordon's Hospital into 'a temporary fort with a garrison of 200 men . . . it was surrounded by a trench, and earthen ramparts, faced with palisadoes and called Fort Cumberland,' so William Kennedy recorded in his *Annals of Aberdeen* of 1818. He added that 400 locals enrolled themselves as a home guard and trained regularly under arms. The attack never came.

The government forces army left Aberdeen on 8 April 1746 and, eight days later, decisively defeated the Jacobites at Culloden. The magistrates later successfully claimed compensation for damage caused at the Doocot Brae and Gordon's Hospital, whose interior appeared to have been kicked to pieces. It had been an uncomfortable six months for Aberdeen as piggy-in-the-middle. While there was considerable support in the North-east for the Jacobite cause at the time of the 1715 Rising, during which the Old Pretender had made a flitting appearance in the area, enthusiasm had waned over the years, and most Aberdonians wanted no part of the Forty-Five. In the years after Culloden, the burgh was able to settle down and get on with business. With the weaving trade in mind, one of the magistrates' earliest plans was to affirm the burgh's ownership of the Denburn Valley and to establish a bleachery there. The 'barrier' of Rosemount Viaduct was yet to be built and the neighbouring districts of Gilcomston, Woolmanhill,

*Mutton Brae with the bridges over the Denburn, leading into the bleachery. Black's Buildings to the left.*

Blackfriars and Schoolhill all stretched further south than they do now and along with the growing settlement of Mutton Brae at the north-east end of the Valley, had sizeable populations of handloom weavers. They had come to the area attracted by low rents and by the Valley itself whose flat bottom, 'the sunken terrace', and ample and accessible water supply from the Denburn had already made it a popular bleachgreen 'common to the people' though the area was still used for rough grazing.

The weavers would have been better served by a professional bleachery with grazing beasts completely banished, for the type of bleaching undertaken by weavers was an integral part of textile production, more complex than simply spreading cloth on the grass and hoping the sun would appear and do the rest. Unless newly woven cloth was intended for the bottom end of the market ie exported for slave wear, it was necessary to bleach it before dyeing and finishing, to remove dirt, seed fragments and the like, and to whiten the cloth which when fresh from the loom was always grey in colour. This was a lengthy, labour-intensive business, involving repeated washing, soaking in an alkaline solution, washing again and drying. Stale urine was also in use. The webs – the newly woven 'squares' from the loom – were pegged out and left for several days to bleach. A nearby water source was essential to this process, which was repeated many times, and took six to eight months or even longer to complete. Only then was the cloth fit for sale. The days of Charles Tennant, the Ayrshire weaver, and his revolutionary bleaching powder (the genesis of ICI) were not yet quite at hand.

Space in bleachfields, with their slow turnover, became hard to secure. And as the town grew, the smaller bleachfields began to vanish. Two were lost in the 1750s, acquired to allow the new hospital at Woolmanhill to expand. At the start of the bleaching season in March 1758 the Town Council feued a piece of ground beside the village of Hardweird in Gilcomston (now under the playground of Gilcomstoun School) to the merchant and Ferryhill farmer Alex Cushnie, 'to be laid out as a Bleachfield.' Indicative of the problems that bleachers were facing was Cushnie's offer of an annual feu duty of 20s, the magistrates noting as they accepted it that this was, 'far above the value.'

A further problem emerged in the 1770s. There was a glut of yarn in the Aberdeen and the Woodside textile mills just north of the city, thanks to the introduction of mechanised spinning. Powered looms had not yet been perfected and yarn, unless twisted very strongly, could not withstand the machine process without snapping. To avoid stockpiling, greater quantities of factory-spun yarn were now being 'put out' for handloom weaving. A contract of co-partnery of November 1785 makes reference to the sale, by Marischal College, of a feu on the west side of Belmont Street at the junction with Schoolhill and close to Mutton Brae. The purchasers were Gordon, Barron & Co, owners of the huge cotton mill, Woodside Works. To deal with their glut of yarn, they now erected their Belmont Street premises, the soon-to-be-infamous Schoolhill Handloom Factory where cotton yarn could be brought in from Woodside and woven into cloth. The site was right and skilled labour was to hand. Meanwhile the Aberdeen magistrates embarked on a campaign to take a part of the Doocot and the whole

*James Duff (1729–1804). The last private owner of the Corbie Heugh.*

Corbie Heugh area on the west side of the Valley into their ownership, to ban grazing, and to create additional bleachfields for the weavers by taking curves out of the serpentine Denburn itself to provide more space.

Alex Cushnie the Ferryhill farmer owned the Doocot Croft and the Corbie Heugh at the time of the Forty-Five, when so much damage was caused by Cope's men. Recompensed for the vandalism at his croftlands, he kept them on for some time after the Rising. But early in 1758 they were acquired by a merchant, John Leslie, who in August of that year sold on to

# THE GREAT BLEACHERY

James Duff, advocate in Aberdeen, its last and its most interesting private owner. He had been a student at King's College and a law apprentice in Aberdeen and a Jacobite rebel in his teens – but by 1758 he was a well-established lawyer and man of business both in Aberdeen and Banff.

\*\*\*

James Duff was the second son of Alexander, second laird of Hatton, near Auchterless in Aberdeenshire. The Duffs were a prominent county family. In 1745 he was sixteen and a student at King's College – students were younger in those days – and at the same time, a writer's (lawyer's) apprentice in Aberdeen. He would have experienced the humiliation suffered in the city during the Cope cantonment in the Corbie Heugh that autumn.

After the Jacobites entered Aberdeen on 25 September, they organised a recruiting drive and young Duff and two friends enlisted and marched to Inverurie with the rebels. Here government troops, mainly McLeods and Munros, sent down from Inverness in an attempt to relieve Aberdeen, were gathering. Principal Chalmers was one of a small group from King's College who had accidentally got caught up in events, and offered their swords, though on the government side.

The Battle of Inverurie, on 23 December 1745, the last pitched battle on North-east soil, was a skirmish with elements of farce. The Jacobites were commanded by the impetuous Lord Lewis Gordon, but stiffened by the Royal Ecossais Regiment. After less than twenty minutes, the hapless government forces – poorly led, lacking knowledge of the lie of the land, and some still in the act of seeking a night's billet – took to their heels and beat a hasty retreat, leaving Inverurie, and indeed the counties of Aberdeen and Banff in Jacobite hands. Principal Chalmers was among the government prisoners. Reports as to their treatment at Jacobite hands vary.

After the battle, James and his friends marched to nearby Keithhall and captured a government supporter, a Mr Maitland of Pitrichy, who was skulking there.

This was something of a coup and the balladeer Charles Leslie, 'Mussel-

Mou'd Charlie', included the incident in his ballad, 'McLeod's Defeat at Inverury':

*Pitrichie hid himself fu' snug*
*Amang a heap o dung man*
*But he was grippit by the Lug*
*Ere morning Bell was rung man*

Alexander Duff and other fathers, who had been much worried during this episode, now exerted influence to have their sons sent home from the Jacobite army. Alarmingly, James Duff had become an entry in Lord Rosebery's 'List of Persons concerned in the Rebellion' as one who 'carried arms in the character of an officer at Inverurie and was one of those who apprehended Mr Maitland of Pitrichy. Not known where he is.' This was serious. Fortunately, after the Battle of Inverurie, the boys' fathers, all gentlemen well affected to George II, were able, through the good offices of Lord Sempill, commanding in Aberdeen, to make contact with Cumberland's aide, the Earl of Albemarle to explain that the boys had been 'seduced to go with the Rebels to Inverurie . . . They are younger brothers and men of no estate or fortune.' Pleas fell on sympathetic ears. No more was heard of the matter and James, who had gone into hiding, reappeared, finished his apprenticeship, completed his studies and graduated. It would be interesting to have had a report of his first encounter with Principal Chalmers after the affray.

He was able to bury his brief Jacobite past and became a successful lawyer, Sheriff Clerk of Banffshire from 1761 and Collector of Assessments to the Commissioners of Supply for Aberdeenshire, posts that would not have been open to anyone with obvious Jacobite sympathies. He did dabble in buying and selling land, but it is unclear why he became involved in the sale of the Corbie Heugh. He was law agent for Mrs Catherine Byron Gordon of Gight, Lord Byron's mother, when she and her son lived in Aberdeen (Gordon heiresses had a clause in their marriage contracts which laid down that the men they married must take the surname of their bride). James Duff's aunt, the formidable Margaret Duff, had married Alexander Gordon,

11th Laird of Gight, and after his death became the Dowager Lady Gight. She was Catherine's grandmother and Lord Byron's great grandmother, and kept an eye on the vulnerable pair.

James Duff married twice and died in 1804. His second son Captain George Duff fell at the Battle of Trafalgar in the following year, while commanding the 74-gun HMS *Mars*.

*** 

James Duff kept the parcel of land for a few months then sold it on to Daniell Cargill, an Aberdeen merchant, not as a private person but to 'Daniell Cargill and his successors in office, Master of the Kirk and Bridge Works of Aberdeen for the use and behoof of the Bridge of Dee charges,' which meant any income from the croft went into the kitty for maintenance of the Bridge of Dee and whatever pertained to it. More importantly, by Duff's disposition to Cargill, the future Union Terrace Gardens came into the hands of the burgh of Aberdeen in 1758 and was recorded in the Burgh Register of Sasines on 3 March 1759.

The land was described as 'that croft tail or piece of land called the Dovecot Brae, comprehending and including also the Corbie Brae (synonymous with the Corbie Heugh) and the rigg of land at the foot of the brae.' Those Doocot lands and the contiguous wooded Corbie Heugh or Brae ran north to Woolmanhill, were bounded by 'the foresaid burn called the Denburn at the east parts,' and took in the whole area across to the railway line, which now runs above the Denburn. That appears to include much of the present Union Terrace Gardens. A less formal account in the Burgh Records dated 23 September 1758 states that: 'That Rigg field presently in Kail and the Brae above the same all along northward from the Dovecot were purchased from Alex Cushnie the proprietor and therefore the council empowers the magistrates to meet with Alex Cushnie's doers [agents] and make the purchase thereof in such reasonable terms as they can agree.' In other words, they were bargaining as to price.

Ownership settled and secured, the Council got on with setting up the Denburn Bleachfield. In that summer of 1758, the Master of the Kirkwork,

Baillie Duncan and the Clerk were instructed 'to see the Denburn streightened [to use the original spelling] and fenced with litter stones, and the bleachfield and road made out.' 'Fenced with litter stones' meant building a drystane dyke with casual stones found lying on the ground or piled on the 'Rubbish Brae', rubbish being the down-takings of old buildings. There were numerous visits of inspection and on 26 September 1758 the councillors returned again to inspect progress at the Denburn, which was still 'presently repairing and straightening.' They 'approved of the work and are unanimously of the opinion that it will be greatly useful for enlarging the bleachfield on the said Burn, and for shutting out all communication of Horses therewith.' To prevent spoiling and damage to the webs, grazing was now taboo. But though horses and cattle were banned from their erstwhile pastures in the Valley, the magistrates had seen to the slaking of their thirst. As the traveller and essayist Francis Douglas, who visited in 1780, wrote in his *Description of the East Coast of Scotland*:

> Just above the bridge, there is a large semi-circular bason (i.e.basin), secured by squared stones on the side and paved with a gentle slope inwards for the convenience of watering horses, or other cattle.

This was also a place where the local young boys gathered to lark around.

Feus continued to be granted after the burn was straightened. On 23 September 1758, William Donaldson, weaver, was granted a feu on the east side of the Denburn: 'as the same is now streightened of the piece of land lying immediately between his house and yard and the new gravel walk on the east side of the Denburn to be allenarly [exclusively] used for a garden or bleachfield but to have no power of ever building any house between these and keeping [blank] feet from the gravel walk and which he is immediately to enclose [ie the garden or bleachfield] and for which he is to pay feu duty.' Nor did the new bleachfields appear to be exclusive to the weavers: 'A bleachfield to be made on one side of the burn for the use of the Inhabitants and a public road on the other side at the expense of the Bridge of Dee charges,' indicating that the bleachfield was available to the general public as well as the professional bleachers. Society had become

# THE GREAT BLEACHERY

*Boys at the 'bason' (the old spelling), the horse trough beside the Bow Brig. Through the arch of Union Bridge is the Corbie Heugh and the houses of Denburn Terrace which were built at the north end. The turreted town house, top left, is No 1-3 Union Terrace. The Monkey House was built on this site.*

more settled, and in some quarters, affluent. Newly woven cloth apart, fine cambric, cotton and linen fabrics were increasingly sought by genteel ladies. All requiring expert bleaching.

Work had gone ahead throughout 1758. Agreement was reached with Robert Joyner with regard to inclosing the bleachfield opposite his land there. Joyner was a tailor, handily placed for offering his services to the weavers. Peter Christie, stocking washer at the Denburn, was granted a feu 'of that piece of vacant ground between Thomas Chasser's yard and the roads leading along the east side of the Denburn, to be used allenarly for a yard or bleachfield and house, and to pay the same feu duty as others in the neighbourhood.' Feus to build houses alone were rare. On 23 September Alexander Henry, farmer at the Denburn, had been granted a feu 'of 30 feet in length and 18 feet in breadth to build a house on the north side of the College Croft, & ascending easterly for which he is to pay at the rate of a penny the foot provided always the said house be lined off and founded at the sight of the Dean of Guild and the Treasurer.' That feu may have been granted for a house because the land was sloping and unsuitable for use as a bleachery. Whatever the case it seems that the measurements and foons (foundations) were to be carefully checked over by the Council's top brass.

In March 1759 there was a serious incident to which the magistrates reacted angrily. 'A nuisance,' that was in the legal sense of causing harm or offence to the public, 'has occurred by scouring stockings in the Denburn above the Bow Bridge whereby the whole cascades built thereon is quite spoiled and the water corrupt so that it will be no manner of use for bleaching linen, besides it will have such a stench that the inhabitants cannot pass or repass. The great expense in straightening the burn and levelling the ground for a bleachfield and Walk will be altogether lost.' Scouring was a particularly vigorous form of cleansing. Chemicals were usually applied, as clearly had happened here, to knitted woollen stockings to remove the natural oiliness of the yarn. The Council ordained that 'after Whitsunday next no person whatsoever shall make a practice of scouring stockings. Intimation is made to the scourers of stockings and other manufacturers that they may take and provide themselves with other courses against Whitsunday next.' The magistrates went on to offer what 'Encouragement as to them shall seem acceptable' to those who had been inconvenienced by this mischanter.

When work on straightening the Denburn's curves and providing additional bleachfields was drawing to a close, the magistrates looked to beautifying as much of the Valley as they could. Francis Douglas continues his account:

> I turned up from the Bow-bridge, and had a very pleasant walk on the Den-Burn. This Den is a deep and broad hollow between two hills [sic] and has a small rivulet in the middle of it. Though its situation and fine shelter pointed it out as a place capable of improvement it lay neglected as a place of common pasture, till the year 1757 when the magistrates at a very considerable expence, made it what it now is.

# THE GREAT BLEACHERY

'A very pleasant walk on the Den-Burn', The watercolour (1840) is by Allan. A dog is being exercised on the gravel walk, singled out by Thomas Pennant, which ran between Schoolhill/ Mutton Brae and the Green. The magistrates were proud of the walk, which in time and somewhat extended mutated into the Denburn dual carriageway. The trees in the Belmont Street back gardens, left, are flourishing, and an elegant clutch of buildings, most of which are still extant, rise up behind them. The South Church, now 'Slains Castle', is extreme left.

On the east side they created a modest pleasance, the sort of pleasure ground that was fashionable among the well-to-do at this time, before the advent of the public park. The Denburn was 'shoed', or given an artificial base and extended to become a little canal. Half-a-dozen or so 'Chinese' bridges were erected but the number diminished over the years. They were possibly inspired by the newly fashionable Willow Pattern china which was based on a Chinese legend of tragic lovers, but designed in Britain and beginning to make its appearance in fashionable salons. With his sharp eye for detail, Douglas wrote:

> From the centre of this pond upward, the stream is confined to a canal about 10 feet wide, the sides of which are lined with cut stones. At short distances the bottom is raised about eighteen inches

and from one division to another, the water falls from a projecting pavement, the whole breadth of the canal. These must have a very pretty appearance when the rivulet is swelled with heavy rains. At different places, wooden bridges in the Chinese taste are thrown over from bank to bank. On the east bank is a broad gravel walk for foot passengers without [outside of] which are many neat buildings. On the west side is a narrower gravel-walk beyond which is an extensive lawn, the common bleachfield of the townspeople.

On the west side, the Council deemed that the braes of Doocot and Corbie should be 'inclosed and fenced and a hedge planted round the top of the same.' This action would lead the way, eventually, to the introduction of the famous balustrades of Union Terrace. John Martin owned the ridge along the top of these braes and it was acquired by the Council in March 1759. Very practically, space was allowed not only for planting the hedge, but 'for digging, dressing and pruning the said hedge.' Martin, a name long associated with the local butcher trade, was granted the right to mow the grass in the 'sunken terrace', and carry it off though he was expressly forbidden 'to carry in any beasts whatsoever within the inclosure to feed on the Grass of the said sunk fences.' And so cows as well as horses were banned from grazing. These were the days before the cattle marts when butchers reared their own beef cattle, so the right to mow the grass and take it away at least allowed Martin to provide fodder for his beasts. In 1760 a person was 'to be employed to take care of the trees, hedges and braes along the canal' – the beginnings of the old Links and Parks Department.

In April 1766 the Council had a bathhouse built over on the east side, accessed by Gaelic Lane and Patagonian Court. 'About the middle of the walk,' wrote Douglas, 'we come up with a large house in which there is a commodious bathing room common to the inhabitants on paying a small gratuity to the person who takes care of it.' At the same time the magistrates instructed repairs 'to secure the shoeing of the canal and the cascades where the same is faulty.' This civic programme of improvement continued during the remainder of the 1760s and the 1770s. The Council ordained that 'the hanging brae the Corbie Heugh upon the west side should be

# THE GREAT BLEACHERY

*Gaelic Lane which runs between Back Wynd and Belmont Street.*

*Patagonian Court. It formed the lower half of the narrow lane running directly from Back Wynd down to the Denburnside and the Bath House. Gaelic Lane was the upper half. They were severed when Belmont Street came through.*

*The bathhouse in the neo-classical style on the banks of the Denburn. The stone piers with finials with woman and child opposite mark the end of Patagonian Court. (A detail from Robert Seaton's painting of Union Bridge, 1807.)*

## THE GREAT BLEACHERY

planted with a proper number of trees. As Douglas commented, 'The side of a steep precipice on the west is planted with trees and shrubs.' The former, likely the elm and ash trees, were planted c.1775. The magistrates also ordained 'that a timber paling should be put up or a sunk fence made along the foot of the said brae and that the Keeper of the Infirmary Bath should be employed to take care of the said plants.' In 1868 James Rettie would write in *Aberdeen 150 Years Ago*: 'Few towns can boast of having in their very centre such a pleasing and agreeable view as is presented looking northward from Union Bridge. The trees which were planted in 1776 have done well, and now form a beautiful contrast to the street east and west of them.' This, it could be argued, was the earliest laying out of Union Terrace Gardens.

At the same time, the Master of Kirk Work and the Dean of Guild were ordered to arch with brick the northmost Chinese bridge. This bridge would have had borne the brunt of the Mutton Brae weaver traffic. The Valley at this time was an interesting blend of the work place and the recreational.

In the 1760s Thomas Pennant, the Welsh gentleman-scholar, writer, antiquarian, zoologist, and generally omniscient in all things to do with natural history, was in Aberdeen amassing material for his *Tour of Scotland*,

*A print of the 1807 painting of Union Bridge, looking south, by Robert Seaton. The Bleachery, with its groups of people and where weavers' webs are either bleaching or pegged out to dry, is almost as dominant as the Bridge. A mother and child cross the Denburn by one of the pack bridges which were thought to be in the Chinese style. They had no parapets and were eventually removed as dangerous. The Bow Brig is in the distance.*

*A detail from Taylor's Map, 1773. We can picture the traveller Thomas Pennant standing beside the 'Bowling Green' and public gardens, top centre, now the extensive forecourt of Robert Gordon's College. The M-shaped little Grammar School is right of the bowling green and above 'Schoolhill'. The original Infirmary at Woolmanhill with its sizeable garden where vegetables were grown is left of Gordon's Hospital (as the College then was). Pennant would have looked straight across to the 'Bleaching Green', the lowest level of the future Union Terrace Gardens. There was no Rosemount Viaduct or Triple Kirks at this time to interfere with his view. The deeper pools in the Denburn, running alongside the bleaching green are marked by a circular motif. 'The Bath' (bathhouse) is across the burn. Only three houses, with their gardens sloping down towards the burn, have been built so far in Belmont Street. The long narrow lane running from below 'Church Yard' to the Denburn gave access to the bath house. The lane survives as Gaelic Lane and Patagonian Court, divided by Belmont Street. Extreme left, centre, a narrow track which became part of the Skene turnpike and gave access to flocks of sheep and to the future Union Terrace Gardens.*

# THE GREAT BLEACHERY

his first collection of travel writings, which was published in 1769. He provides a wider glimpse of the area around the future Union Terrace Gardens. We can picture him standing at the foot of the pubic bowling green at Robert Gordon's Hospital, and looking around him, notebook in hand. No Triple Kirks in those days and of course no Rosemount Viaduct. This is what he saw and wrote:

> The grammar school is a low but neat building. Gordon's Hospital is handsome; in front is a good statue of the founder; it maintains forty boys, children of the inhabitants of Aberdeen who are apprenticed at proper ages. The infirmary is a large plain building, and sends out between eight and nine hundred cured patients annually. On the side of the Great Bleachery, which is common to the town, are the public walks.

The 'low but neat' Grammar School (1757–1863) was not the first of that name in Schoolhill, but it was the immediate predecessor of the present school in Skene Street. It sat directly above 'Schoolhill' on Taylor's map and the original Gray's School of Art was later built on its site. It is commemorated by a plaque that is as modest as the school once was. Lord

*The little Grammar School where Byron was a pupil. The original Gray's School of Art was built on this site in 1885 before moving to Garthdee in 1967.*

Byron, when plain George Gordon, was a pupil there between 1795 and 1798, and would have known the Corbie Heugh well. It lay only a stone's throw away. The Grammar School provided a classical education for the sons of local gentry and the professional classes, whereas Gordon's Hospital was not a hospital in the sense of curing the sick, but a charitable institution, founded to educate the sons of indigent burgesses and the genteel poor and had a broader, more vocational curriculum than the Grammar, including English, French, arithmetic, book-keeping, navigation, singing and a little Latin. But it was not a school for street loons: it became Robert Gordon's College in 1881. The 'good statue of the founder,' in marble by John Cheere, was originally positioned in a custom-built niche over the frontage in 1753.

Pennant notes a 'large, plain infirmary' beside the Well of Spa at Woolmanhill. This was not Archibald Simpson's elegant essay in

*The artist Jackson Simpson's interpretation of how the original hospital at Woolmanhill might have looked.*

# THE GREAT BLEACHERY

*A discussion is underway at the Corbie Well.*

neo-classicism of the 1830s, but its predecessor of 1742, chosen because of 'the goodness of the air of the place' and the proximity of the healing well. Among its earliest patients were wounded McLeods and Munroes from the Battle of Inverurie of December 1745, while in April 1746 it was occupied by government soldiers who had been wounded at Culloden. Too small from the start, additional wings were added in 1755 and 1758. A cow provided milk for the patients, which may occasionally have been herded across to the Denburn Valley in the days when rough grazing was allowed, and when the hospital garden required some respite. Pennant would have seen the Denburn Valley and the bleachfield when he looked across the Schoolhill. He has nothing to say about the Chinese bridges or the burn's cascades. Instead he notes the public walks which are 'on the side of the Great Bleachery, which is common to the town.'

Life in and around the Denburn Valley was hard, but peaceful and friendly, except among the highly territorial local gangs of loons, taking their gang names from the places where they lived. 'The great event of boy life in the district,' recalled the journalist Robert Anderson in *Aberdeen in Bygone Days*

(1910), 'were the battles between the "Mutton Braes" and the "Corbies" from the Corbie Well area, the "Well of Spa Boys" from Woolmanhill, the "Bow Brig" boys from around the Bow Brig, and the "Green Linties" who came up from the Green.' The more peaceful womenfolk would have had exchange of gossip in the mornings round the Corbie Well, which at this time stood in the Corbie Heugh, at the railing which separated the Heugh from the bleachgreen. There were friendly gatherings of an evening when locals from Mutton Brae, Woolmanhill, Schoolhill and Blackfriars, perhaps even Gilcomston, met for a gossip: the men smoking their pipes, the women knitting shanks for Baillie Hadden and his fellow wool merchants. The arrival of power looms that worked efficiently brought this Indian summer of the handloom weavers to an end. By the 1830s, weavers made redundant by mechanised weaving in the mills and by the closure of the Schoolhill handloom factory were leaving the area in search of work. The Great Bleachery, though still popular with domestic bleachers, was less busy, and there were far fewer weavers' webs bleaching on the grass or hanging out to dry.

Chapter Three

# FROM THE CORBIE HEUGH TO UNION TERRACE GARDENS

As the nineteenth century wore on, the character of the Denburn Valley began to change. When weaving became automated, the handloom weavers left to seek work elsewhere and the great webs, slowly turning from

A magnificent, romanticised oil painting of the Denburn Valley before Union Terrace Gardens. The view is 'From Woolmanhill looking south, 1862'. To the left are Mutton Brae and the Triple Kirks and in the centre the Denburn flows towards Union Bridge. Corbie Heugh is on the right.

grey to white gradually vanished, to be replaced by smaller, more colourful domestic garments. The Denburn with its deep circular pools had been a popular spot for washing clothes but with the initiation of the Cairnton water supply on Deeside by Queen Victoria in October 1866, the washing of clothes at the burnside became a thing of the past. In any case, the water of the Denburn, which served many masters during its six-mile journey from Kingswells, had become polluted by the dyeworks and tanneries upstream of the Great Bleachery. Old people remembered when there had been trout in the burn, but these were replaced by less discriminating bandies, then by eels and then by loch leeches. The cascades were neglected and the dangerous little Chinese bridges deteriorated and were replaced but only where provision of a crossing was essential. No matter, for stretches of the burn within the Valley would presently be covered in, first piecemeal, then completely to allow for the building of the Denburn Valley Junction Railway. The bathhouse, an increasingly dilapidated survivor from the era of the pleasure ground, reached the end of its days.

Like the Denburn, the Corbie Heugh across on the west side became another problem place though, for a start, things went well. Union Terrace was being laid out, running northward from the junction with Union Street, opposite the top of the Corbie Heugh or the Planted Bank, as it was now called. The old name was being supplanted by a clutch of more dignified appellations which succeeded each other at amazing speed. The 'Plantation', 'the Union Terrace Plantation', 'the Wooded Slopes' and others were tossed about. For a time, 'the Wooded Bank' emerged as favourite before 'the Denburn Gardens' took over. The Town Council allowed the new proprietors and their tenants the right to walk there by a grant of 'servitude and liberty.' They also forbade any building work on the east side of the new terrace and between the terrace and the Denburn, ie in the Valley. Feuars therefore enjoyed excellent views of the rural scene opposite and the value of the feus increased. Union Terrace came to a halt at right angles to Skene Terrace, handily opposite a pub. Skene Terrace carried on down towards Woolmanhill, but a gap between the pub and a neighbouring house allowed pedestrian access to Skene Street just beyond. Union Terrace was a cul-de-sac, a private and privileged place.

*Wood's Plan, 1821. Union Terrace has not yet been straightened out, and the Corbie Heugh alongside is still thickly wooded. The north end is bounded by 'Chapel Street' (Wood means Skene Terrace), though Denburn Terrace has already sneaked in. Its long gardens stretch to the Denburn at Mutton Brae where there are outhouses and washing. 'G' is the old Grammar School sitting at the front of Gordon's Hospital. The long building standing alone well to the left of the Grammar could be the Schoolhill handloom factory. The outlines of the Mutton Brae settlement are above 'Denburn'.*

Unfortunately, as early as 1815, the Plantation was showing signs of neglect, so the Town Council decided on a new system which was aimed at producing more revenue, and a tidier Plantation at no cost to themselves. The Belmont Street proprietors whose back gardens descended to the Denburnside were brought into the arrangement and given equal rights with the Union Terrace proprietors to walk in the wooded slopes of the Plantation, which was to be enclosed. The proprietors were to be responsible for laying the ground out 'in a neat and proper manner with paths, plantings and shrubberies, and maintain it in all time coming as a pleasure ground' for themselves. They were to bear all costs. It was also agreed that if the Plantation fell into a neglected state again, the Town Council would have the power to take over and charge the proprietors for the work done. During the nineteenth century little wars rumbled on spasmodically between Aberdeen Town Council and the Union Terrace proprietors who were represented by Messrs Lumsden & Robertson (sometimes Robertson & Lumsden), advocates, of No. 3 Union Terrace over the state of the former Heugh. Complaints from the residents continued for years. Many were over the condition of the Plantation's railings. One long railing had divided the Corbie Heugh off from the bleachery, while at the top, the ugly railing that bounded the Corbie Heugh Plantation on its west side with Union Terrace had long been a target of vandals. One prank was to remove the spikes from the railings and liability for their repair or replacement was a longstanding bone of contention between the feuars and the Council.

Early in the nineteenth century, Denburn Terrace – a row of tenemental

*The upper railings which divided Union Terrace from the Corbie Heugh, the cause of much annoyance. The Northern Assurance offices/Monkey House extreme left. The neat heaps by the kerb could be manure awaiting collection for the Dung Stance in King Street.*

houses with long front gardens, attractive to look at in the old prints – had made its appearance below the Corbie Heugh, starting off from the vulnerable northern end where access was easy. Its residents were of a respectable class and included a chemical light manufacturer, a clerk, butcher, beadle, teacher, cabinetmaker and midwife. Its location as originally planned, 'Skene Terrace to Union Bridge,' was ambitious: virtually the entire length of the future Gardens. Had Denburn Terrace progressed that far, one suspects there would never have been a Union Terrace Gardens. As it was, its outhouses and washing lines extended across the Valley, and are visible in old prints of Mutton Brae as is the occasional mean-looking house. Following the Denburn Terrace example, jobbing builders would have filled the Valley with more houses. Fortunately the Terrace did not progress further than the Corbie Well, at that time about half way along the old Corbie Heugh/Plantation, at the foot of the Valley. A row of houses had also appeared at the north-east end of Union Terrace, parallel to Denburn Terrace, regardless of the embargo on building there. A few back houses had even gone up in the space between the two terraces, in spite of the difference in levels. The old idea of seclusion as a means of increasing the value of the Union Terrace feus had gradually gone by the board. Control over the development of the Denburn Valley appeared to be in abeyance.

The Playe Greene, the Woolmanhill and the Four Neukit Garden had been built over long years before. Simpson's handsome Infirmary, which had replaced the earlier cottage hospitals in the 1830s, was surrounded by timber yards, granite yards, combworks and joiners' workshops. With the disappearance of the ancient 'leisure and recreation' area and the covering in of parts of the Denburn and Gilcomston Burn, the northern boundary of the Valley was vague. Turning to the east bank, a little group of houses, still shabbily picturesque, was all that was left of Mutton Brae after the railway was constructed. Most of the weavers had gone and the Brae had become home to a small colony of pawnbrokers and chimney sweeps. At the south end, the Valley had been dominated since the early nineteenth century by the gigantic yet graceful Union Bridge.

By 1863 the brilliant architect James Matthews (1819–1898), designer of the palatial new Grammar School and then in his forties, was in his first

# UNION TERRACE GARDENS

This illustration of the Denburn Valley looking north is dated 1863, just one year after the idyllic painting of the same area looking south, and two years before the railway came. Here the Denburn is at its ugliest, the bleach greens drab, the gravel walk, once the pride of the councillors, worn and weary. Its name had changed from the rural-sounding Denburnside to the urban Lower Denburn Road. The entry to Patagonian Count is lower right but the bathhouse has gone. Some of the back gate piers have lost their ball finials and the trees of the Belmont Street back gardens look scraggy. The last house, upper right, is about to be demolished to make way for Belmont Street Congregational Church (later St Nicholas, now the Priory). Left is the Corbie Heugh/Wooded Bank et alia and the lower fence, and to the north an ominous agglomeration of buildings, from left, Denburn Terrace, Skene Terrace, Black's Building and Mutton Brae. Woolmanhill Hospital hovers above. The Triple Kirks (1843-1844) look like a giant rocket about to zoom off to some better place. The wooden bridge with the distinctive parapet, seen in the idyllic painting, features again. This is the place that James Matthews was determined to turn into a public park. It could so easily have become a large colony of poor housing.

*James Matthews. He looks like the young architectural visionary that one would expect: intelligent, determined, perhaps a little apprehensive.*

period as an Aberdeen town councillor. He cared passionately about the Corbie Heugh area and perhaps had played there as a boy. He would have heard family stories about how his maternal grandfather, the architect William Ross, had taken over the construction of Union Bridge when the first team of architects received their marching orders, owing to mistakes in levels and estimates. Ross, at that time contractor for the Aberdeenshire Canal, undertook to build the bridge for £9,816. 'The contract was signed on 2 December 1802,' wrote Robert Anderson in *Aberdeen in Bygone Days*, 'and so rapidly was the work prosecuted that the keystone of the arch was driven on 25 August 1803.'

Matthews had been educated at Robert Gordon's Hospital and in 1834 was articled to the great Archibald Simpson, where he worked under the supervision of Simpson's assistant, Thomas Mackenzie, who was five years his senior. At the age of twenty, Matthews travelled to London where he gained further experience as assistant to George Gilbert Scott, then in the early days of his prolific and distinguished architectural career – which at a later date, appears to have included the destruction of the medieval ceiling of St Machar's Cathedral. He returned to Aberdeen in 1844, where Archibald Simpson, recognising his talents, offered him a senior assistantship with the promise of a partnership. Matthews declined. Apparently he thought Simpson would be 'too greedy.' Instead he went into partnership with Simpson's former assistant, his old boss, Thomas Mackenzie, who attended to the Elgin office, while Matthews remained in Aberdeen. Simpson himself died in 1847.

Matthews' ability and originality were soon recognised. In 1847, his St Nicholas Poorhouse became the model for all future poorhouses in Scotland, although the building itself, near the old bed of the Aberdeenshire Canal, had subsidence problems. In 1858 he designed the large auditorium which overnight turned the Assembly Rooms seamlessly into the Music Hall; the Town & County Bank in Aberdeen, and many others elsewhere followed.

In the Corbie Heugh he found agreements on its maintenance 'more honoured in the breach than in the observance' the trees and shrubs there dead, dying, overcrowded, impassable and generally neglected. The need to replace them with more varied foliage was overdue but neither the Council nor the proprietors would accept responsibility.

Fortunately, not only did Matthews have a vision, but also something of his grandfather's drive and tenacity. In 1868, a few months after the completion of the Denburn Valley Junction Railway, he made what at the time must have seemed an astonishing proposal. He suggested that 'the whole of Union Terrace be turned into a pleasure ground for the people' by which he meant the old Corbie Heugh area in its entirety across to the new railway line. Public parks, it is true, were becoming popular, for fresh air and exercise were highly commended. The city's first, if you discount Jamesone's Four Neukit Garden, would be the Victoria Park of 1871, created from the thirteen acres of Glennie's Parks (fields), grazing ground out at the Low Stocket. But that was flat ground and virtually in the country. But having a park in uneven terrain in what had become a busy central area associated with work rather than leisure, whose burn with its cascades and Chinese bridges had been replaced by a railway with steam trains belching smoke and soot, where, nevertheless, some housewives and servants still used the bleachgreen in the centre, whose old Corbie Heugh had become a jungle, with controversy and vandalism on the west side, and encroaching houses at the north end must have seemed a curious notion. But in view of the insidious advance of housing, Matthews' proposal was not a moment too soon. It helped that the Provost, Alexander Nicol, was also was keen to have 'a pleasant little park.' Discussion got underway in the Council, and in the town, generally. As Anderson put it, 'When aesthetic notions began to prevail, the propriety of utilising the picturesque site of the Wooded Bank to better advantage was repeatedly advocated.'

Ideas on improving the environment and facilitating movement around the whole area were aired in that same year. A Special Committee on Improvements was appointed to consider whether the open space in front of Union Terrace and along the Upper Denburn 'cannot be so improved as to increase the amenity of those residing in the immediate vicinity and conducive to the recreation of the inhabitants generally, and at the same time open a carriage communication with Skene Street.' Much more would be heard of that latter proposal, which meant making the narrow Union

Terrace a through-road. Environmental issues and town planning were, it seemed, at last being taken seriously.

In 1869, the year after Matthews announced his surprising proposal for a 'pleasure ground for the people,' a plan entitled 'Sketch of the Proposed Denburn Gardens' was drawn up by the land surveyor James Forbes Beattie – presumably at Matthews' suggestion. It would greatly influence the eventual layout of what became Union Terrace Gardens. Beattie had a feeling for landscape, and the plan was expertly contoured to the awkward lie of the land (Beattie's plans and life in general are looked at in more detail in the next chapter). Eventually, in February 1872 after much procrastination, the Town's Improvements Committee asked James Matthews to prepare a report on the laying out of the Denburn Valley as a public park – the idea he had mooted four years earlier. By that time he had resigned from the Town Council and was devoting more time to his private practice, though he attended relevant Committee meetings at the Town House.

Things were also moving with regard to public ownership of 'the said Plantation or Planted Bank' or 'Wooded Slope' – our old friend the Corbie Heugh. In March 1872, the Improvements Committee approved a draft contract between Aberdeen Town Council and the proprietors on Union Terrace and the west side of Belmont Street drawn up by their lawyers, Messrs Lumsden & Robertson, that they should continue to have their right to walk upon 'the said Plantation' but now to be shared and enjoyed by the public. The proprietors agreed to contribute a one-off payment of £100 towards the necessary repairs, improvements and a new layout for the Plantation. This seemed another step towards creating a public park, but there were more delays. Some months later Baillie Esslemont asked what had been done in regard to the Wooded Bank (the latest name for the Plantation/Corbie Heugh) for there was continuing vandalism 'and the place was being destroyed rapidly.' The Lord Provost commented that he had attended a meeting of the feuars involved which had to be adjourned 'because the feuars had temporarily declined to sign.' This business of 'declining to sign' was repeated on a number of occasions.

Matthews' report, reiterating and expanding on his earlier ideas, was presented on 5 August 1872. It included the throwing open of the whole ground between the Wooded Bank and the railway wall as far up as a (proposed) new light iron bridge, to create a pleasure ground and the erection of that iron bridge to take pedestrians across the Denburn Valley from Woolmanhill to Union Terrace. The bridge marked the northern end of the recreation ground and was perhaps also designed as a barrier against further incursions from speculative builders. The report also mooted the removal of the long railing at the foot of the Wooded Bank, while the flat portion of ground at the north end was 'to be laid out for bowling or croquet greens. The Wooded Bank could be intersected by walks, planted with evergreens and properly sloped and sown with grass.'

It was necessary to remove the bleachgreen, but, as it is 'a convenience to many persons,' Matthews noted, 'I propose to form a new bleachgreen, north of the new bridge.' Covering in a remaining stretch of open Denburn in the area was necessary as 'a most disagreeable effluvia' was arising from it. The Corbie Well was to be fitted up with a polished granite fountain. The laying out of walks, bowling and croquet greens* were 'to be put under the direction of a tastefully and competent Landscape Gardener.' This was probably Mr Robert Walker, keeper of the new Victoria Park, who was down 'to give assistance.' These were far-sighted and pioneering proposals and Matthews' estimated the costs at £1,735. He took the Improvements Committee on a site visit. They generally approved of his report and plan but decided they should only proceed with the repair of the iron railings along Union Terrace, and have the Wooded Bank properly enclosed where the fence had been broken down near the Corbie Well. Matthews had hoped to have this area thrown open.

He must have been disappointed that his far-reaching proposals met with such a timid response. But he was accustomed to the ways of the Town Council who tended to see the smaller picture and were obsessional about railing and fences, and it was always a start. In due course the iron railings were repaired by William McKinnon & Co., iron founders, for £60, and the stone base by James Willox for £16 10s. Watson & Robb repaired the fence at the Corbie Well for £86 12s.

* The bowling and croquet greens seem not to have materialised.

Things continued to progress but at the usual speed – dead slow. Back at the Wooded Bank, the old Corbie Heugh, which the Council had now contracted to maintain, the proprietors were in revolt. In October 1873 Mr Angus, the Town Clerk, read out an angry letter from Messrs Robertson & Lumsden about the Council's tardiness in attending to its overgrown state. Unless a satisfactory assurance was received that there would be no further delay in carrying out the Council's undertaking 'we shall deem it necessary to send a copy of our correspondence to the newspapers that the public may know that the blame of the disgraceful state in which the Bank still is does not lie with the proprietors.' Arguments continued for a considerable time with the feuars over the improvement of the Wooded Bank. Nothing came of that for the time being, nor from the 'considerable amount of interest' raised in 1875 to have a drive laid out along the Union Terrace Wooded Bank to the Skene Street Bridge (Collie's Brig, at the foot of the street). This would make Union Terrace a through-road. The Police Committee rather sheepishly recommended that no action be taken 'on account of the difficulty with which the carrying out of such a scheme would be attended.'

At last overcoming their preference for procrastination, the Town Council by early 1876 had taken up Matthews' proposal that the ground between the Wooded Bank and the railway be turned into a pleasure ground; the Wooded Bank be properly sloped and planted; the bleachgreen be transplanted and the Denburn covered in as suggested. Mr Robert Walker was placed in charge and Matthews took the Improvements Committee on a site visit. They generally approved of his report, but again there was much procrastination both by his Council colleagues and difficult residents where negotiations for the acquisition of property added to the delay. Eventually Matthews' literally groundbreaking proposals were adopted. The enthusiasm of the councillors grew and they began to take a 'hands on' approach, personally testing the gradients of the slopes and reporting those which were too steep. Proposals were made on improving the gradients of the centre and north walks and the strengthening of railings. It was all done by spade, pickaxe and a small fleet of wheelbarrows. Steps were taken to ensure that a wall at the railway boundary would not be so high as to obscure the view of the Gardens enjoyed by railway passengers.

# FROM THE CORBIE HEUGH TO UNION TERRACE GARDENS

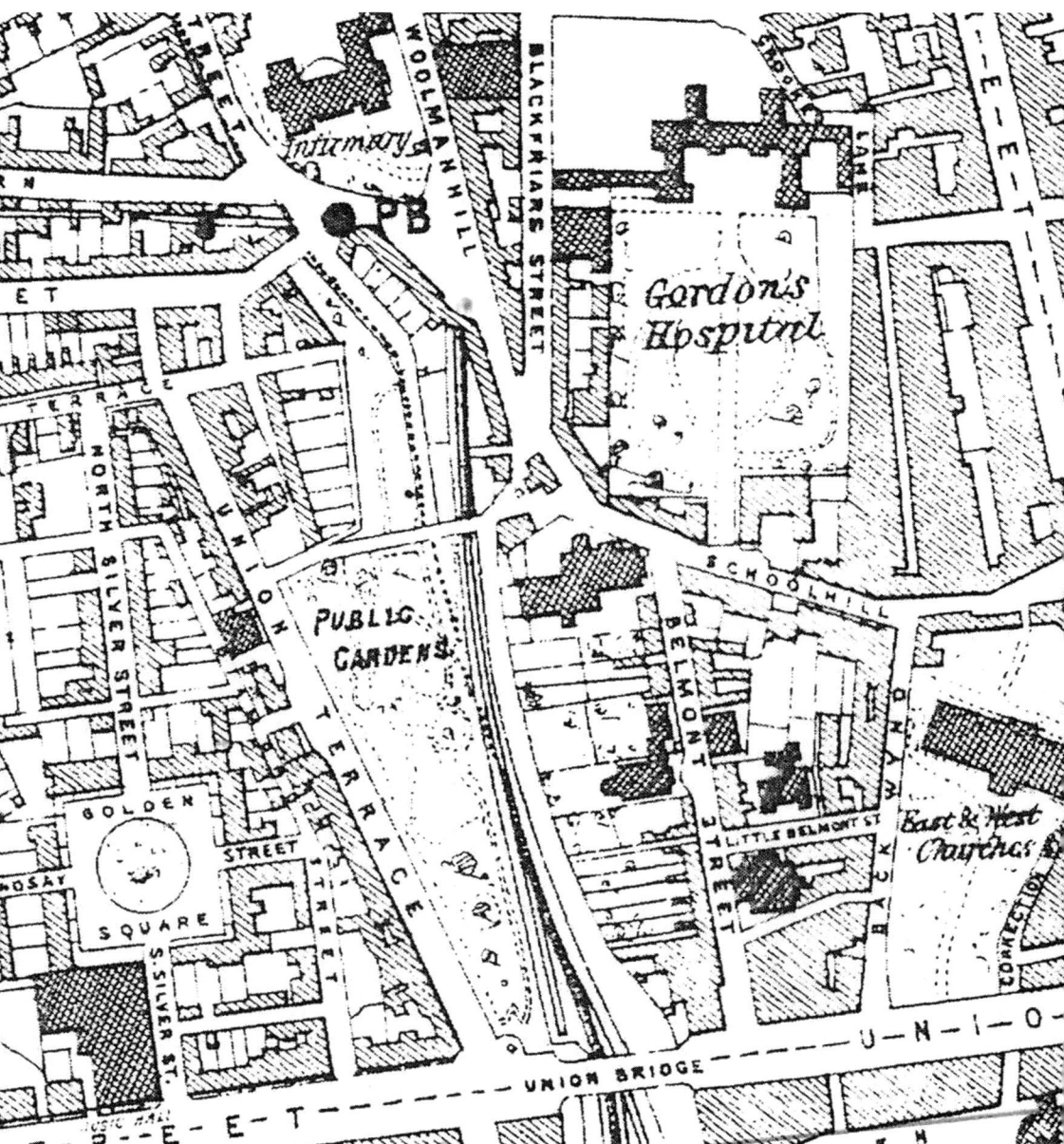

*Matthews' work at the north end of the 'Public Gardens' (UTG) is cut out for him. Beyond the light iron bridge, Denburn Terrace with its long gardens dominates, but some land to the east has been ceded from the railway. There are houses on the east side of Union Terrace. The Triple Kirks are above and left of Belmont Street and Gordon's Hospital, above, was about to become Gordon's College. The Grammar School sits in public garden above 'Schoolhill'. The Infirmary at Woolmanhill, left above, has pavilions added to the rear. Detail from the Aberdeen Post Office Map of 1880.*

*Union Terrace Gardens, looking north in the early 1880s. The iron footbridge, and the bandstand are in place, the latter arriving c1880. The path on the left, resembling a chute, needs steps. It is overhung by trees for this is the last outpost of the Corbie Heugh. Right of the chute are the tenemental houses of Denburn Terrace. Skene Terrace blocks the north end. A few people are in the park and on the bridge. Not much sign yet of flower-beds though there are some saplings in the foreground and the enduring urns appear. The replacement bleaching green can be spotted to the north.*

On 7 February 1877, the Town Council entered into a treaty of excambion (land exchange) with the Great North of Scotland Railway (GNSR) under which the Council acquired two pieces of land below Mutton Brae, and the GNSR a piece of land at Union Bridge. This was a good 'deal'. Acquiring land below Mutton Brae allowed the clearance of unsightly sheds and

washing lines while the disposal of a shadowy spot 'almost shut off from the sun's rays by the high ground of Union Street' allowed the GNSR to construct the famous turntable. In that year, the light iron footbridge with a handsome wrought iron parapet and granite supports was at last built across the Denburn Valley Railway Line at the north end of the Gardens, just as in Beattie's 'Sketch' (page 62). The lowest tender had been accepted, that of Adam Mitchell & Co at £1,000 (Mitchell, a well-known master mason and councillor who had built the Grammar School to Matthews' plans had died just before the contract was confirmed). 'The iron work (of the bridge) is elaborately ornamental and the whole structure is light and graceful in appearance,' reported *The Aberdeen Journal*. The ironwork for the Gardens including new railings was to be made by Blaikie Bros at a cost of £830.

In that same year of 1877, Matthews provided detailed plans for the widening of Union Terrace 'from 5 feet to 30 feet,' *The Aberdeen Journal* reported, which included 'a broad pavement, to be laid out along the side next to the Gardens.' This widening operation left a drop of 17 feet between pavement and Gardens and as Matthews said, 'as a dead wall would have a most unpleasant effect, we recommend that this part be bridged across by three stone arches. Under these arches the face of the bank would make an excellent fernery and rockery and if so utilised might make a very interesting feature.' The three arches eventually developed into the twenty or so which form the long arcade, one of the Gardens' most striking features.

Union Terrace Gardens opened to the public in the summer of 1878. The name was an automatic choice and had been used informally for some time. No more Corbie Heugh, Wooded Bank, Planted Bank and all the rest of them – nor even Denburn Gardens nor Denburn Meadows, which were the most appropriate, but the word 'Denburn' sent out the wrong message. That was a pity, for in a bland way, 'Union Terrace Gardens' evokes douce flower-beds fronting a row of terraced houses. The concept of Corbie Heugh – the 'Cliff of the Crows' – on the other hand had become a trifle wild for a city-centre park. But children from working-class homes in the neighbourhood now had a splendid playground in the heart of the city and gave it their own name. They called it Trainie Park.

The Union Terrace Gardens of 1877 was about 80 per cent of the size of the present Gardens. There was still land in the north to be tamed. Matthews' work was by no means over.

Chapter Four

# JAMES FORBES BEATTIE: THE FORGOTTEN DESIGNER OF UNION TERRACE GARDENS

*James Forbes Beattie*

James Forbes Beattie and James Matthews went back a long way. They were in complementary professions and they covered the same territory, though in addition to their North-east clientele Beattie had also a sizeable client base in the Mearns, Matthews in the Highlands.

In 1864 both men were working at Brotherton House in Kincardineshire, then under construction. Matthews, recently elected to Aberdeen Town Council, was the architect and Beattie the landscape architect. Matthews likely took the opportunity to discuss his ideas for a public park in the Corbie Heugh with his colleague. In 1868, Matthews presented his plans for the park to his fellow councillors. Within months Beattie had surveyed the area and drawn up, with considerable skill, a plan which he modestly entitled 'A Sketch of proposed Denburn Gardens, combining Foot Bridge with Sewerage Works, 1869'.

Like Matthews, Beattie carried a vast workload, appears to have had much stamina, did not fuss, was modest, quick and efficient – but who was he? Some time ago I mentioned his name to Historic Scotland who commented, 'Union Terrace Gardens appears to have been (his) only public park commission. However, this in itself is not significant given the modest scale and simplicity of the gardens combined with the fact the Beattie is not particularly celebrated at national level.' This latter comment is certainly true! In his time he was perhaps the most able and sought-after surveyor, landscape architect, garden designer and civil engineer in Scotland, and, since he devised the original plan for Union Terrace Gardens this is the very place to celebrate him.

James Forbes Beattie, the second of three sons, was born around 1802 in the Aberdeenshire village of Insch. Surprisingly, given that his father was the local GP, there is some vagueness as to his exact year of birth. But Beattie senior was a busy man. As well as being a popular and capable physician, he was also tenant farmer of Dunideer and clerk to the county road trustees. Clearly a lad o' pairts.

Following in their father's footsteps, his eldest son succeeded to the family farm and became a progressive and prosperous farmer while the youngest became a GP and a director of P&O and other companies. James, the middle son, went a separate route. He attended classes at Marischal College and then was articled to David Walker, a well-known surveyor and civil engineer in Aberdeen. Having been apprentice and assistant, Beattie was taken into partnership after five years with the firm which in 1829 became Walker & Beattie. David Walker appreciated his energy, accuracy and commitment. Civil Engineering, an ancient skill, had by this time separated from military engineering and was coming into its own. Beattie had timed his arrival well. A Royal Charter of 1828 formally recognised the profession, and Beattie could add the initials CE after his name, no doubt with pride.

His early commissions included laying out the grounds and gardens of Belmont, a handsome house at Kittybrewster close to the new Aberdeen marts – now only evoked in the street name, Belmont Road – and preparing an estate plan for the Leslies of Balquhain near Inverurie. In 1836 he married Jane Copland, daughter of the Aberdeen Town Clerk Depute. Perhaps two or even all three of their children – two sons and a daughter – would have been born 'down under', for in 1838 the Beatties sailed for Australia. Beattie had decided on a major career change, and had been appointed manager of the Kaawa Copper Mining Company which was owned by a consortium of Aberdeen merchants.

Beattie had accumulated a little money during his years in Australia, and when the family returned to Aberdeen some ten years later he was able to acquire No. 2 Bon Accord Square in the city's prestigious business-cum-residential quarter. Here he established his office as land surveyor, valuator and civil engineer, and set up house there as well. He recommenced where he had left off nearly a decade earlier, drawing up plans for estate farms at Balquhain and at nearby Fetternear. Public work offered many opportunities for surveyors at this time and soon after his return he was appointed Assistant Commissioner for Scotland under Sir Robert Peel's Drainage Act of 1842 and Inspector for the Enclosure Commissioners under the General Enclosure Act of 1845. He was also responsible for paying out grants for the reclamation work that ensued from this relatively recent legislation. It was estimated that a quarter of a million pounds, a vast sum in those days, had passed through his hands in grant aid. One result was the appearance of many fine stone farmhouses and steadings in the North-east on recovered land, not a few of them designed by Beattie himself.

His work on the Aberdeenshire turnpikes also fell into the public domain and in 1849 he supervised repairs and alterations to the Skene Turnpike. The downhill section adjacent to Rubislaw Quarry in particular was prone to damage from heavy wagons loaded with blocks of granite. The following year he drew up a feuing plan for the Rubislaw estate which lies in the vicinity of the Quarry. He was much taken with the beauty and solitude of the still undeveloped Rubislaw Den, through which the Denburn flows en route to the Denburn Valley, and he and his family became the sole residents in 1851. The Den must have been a splendid adventure playground for the young Beatties.

The 1867 Ordnance Survey of Rubislaw Den shows terraces stretching to about 500 yards east of the sole residence, a Georgian mansion, Rubislawden House. These terraces could have been the work of an itinerant Italian gardener employed by Beattie's predecessor, Sheriff Dauney, the Den's first resident, but they could have been laid out and were almost certainly expanded by Beattie, experimenting with a style that he would later use so memorably for Union Terrace Gardens. At some point he may also have designed the terraced gardens at Ecclesgreig House near Montrose where he eventually met his fate.

In 1854 he was faced with a momentous task. For over 100 years, lairds whose lands were adjacent to Bennachie had quarrelled over rights to the famous Aberdeenshire hill, in pasturage, casting peats, quarrying granite and particularly of shooting game and dealing with the question of the 'squatters'. The eight lairds in dispute at this time included Col. Leslie of Balquhain, Lord Forbes of Castle Forbes, Sir James Grant of Monymusk and Col. Erskine of Pittodrie. Beattie was well known to them all, and all were willing to come to arbitration, provided that Beattie were arbiter. The Court of Session instructed him 'to undertake the division of the Commonty of Bennachie, perambulate and go over the whole Commonty with a view to ascertaining the quality of its different parts . . .' to lodge a scheme of division and subsequently 'to set march stones and cairns for the division and to set the peat mosses.' In a remarkably short space of time, Beattie divided and apportioned the Commonty of over 4,042 acres. His work had been arduous, both physically and mentally. It was a testimony to his skill and expertise that these powerful and argumentative men accepted his findings with only minor quibbles (the saga of the Bennachie Colonists and their struggles with the lairds came later).

This was the era of the Big House and, throughout his career, Beattie was much in demand for designing and laying out the grounds of estates, and the gardens of great houses in Aberdeenshire, Kincardineshire, Banffshire, Caithness, Fife and in Perthshire, where he laid out the gardens of Dall and Balthayock Houses. Not all have survived. Some will still recall Balnagask House, once the family home of the Davidsons of Balnagask, in its later life, as an old folks' home in Torry. It dated from the 1820s and in Beattie's day lay quite isolated in Kincardineshire. Here he created a splendid garden encompassing a motte, and laid out a tree-lined carriage drive which led down to the harbour. It is now Baxter Street, Torry.

Beattie's most prestigious client was the Royal Family. Prince Albert had purchased the Balmoral Estate in 1852, having been inspired by the new Trinity Hall in Aberdeen's Union Street. 'Who is the architect of this fine building?' he had asked when driving past, en route for the first time from the harbour to Balmoral Old House. On hearing it was John Smith, the Aberdeen city architect, Albert commissioned him to design the new Balmoral Castle that he and Queen Victoria were contemplating. John Smith died before work could start, but his son, William, who had assisted his father on the Trinity Hall project, designed Balmoral Castle according to Prince Albert's wishes. The Royals valued their privacy and the picturesque bridge, marking the boundary with the neighbouring estate of Invercauld, passed too close to the new Castle for comfort. In 1859 Beattie was summoned to Balmoral and commissioned to design and built the new Invercauld Bridge. Old Invercauld Bridge was closed off but still has a life, featuring on picture postcards and being admired by tourists. Beattie also laid out the grounds and designed the gardens at Balmoral, where before there had been 'nothing but wilderness,' as well as laying out private roads on the estate including the Queen's Drive from Crathie around Loch Muick to Altnaguibhsaich Lodge (The Hut) and linking it with the remote Glas Alt Sheil. Correspondence between Prince Albert and James Forbes Beattie is preserved in the Royal Archives at Windsor.

Beattie's career was many-sided. He designed and was involved in the management of the cruive dykes (salmon traps) for the River Don Salmon Fishings and brought in a water supply to several Aberdeenshire villages. He laid out new cemeteries for the North-east parishes of Turriff and Old Deer. He managed the Fife Estates Improvement Bill (the Broomhall Estate of the Earls of Elgin) which were continually in a state of financial crisis. He was one of the most energetic and efficient directors of the North of Scotland Bank – as was James Matthews – and sole valuator for many of the new railway undertakings in the north, including the Great North of Scotland Railway. This was a full-time career in itself.

Just prior to his death Beattie was involved in a massive three-sided project. Firstly he drew up plans for a modern suburb at Ruthrieston, an ancient settlement at the Bridge of Dee, one of the entrances to Aberdeen; secondly he completed plans for a grand new entrance to the city, a carriage drive later named Riverside Drive. Part of the route would be flanked by

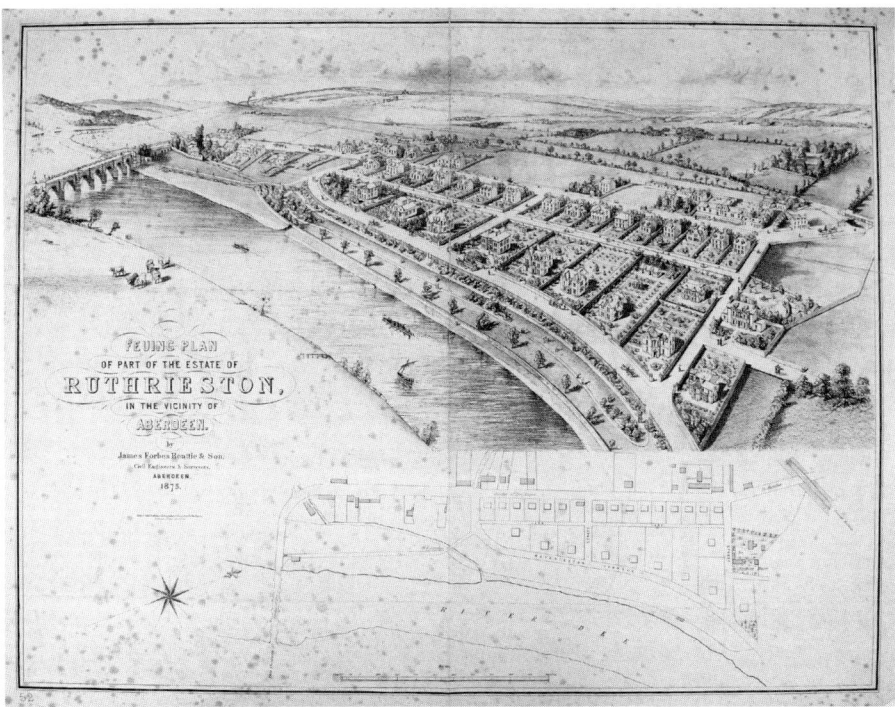

*Beattie's feuing plan for the new suburb of Ruthrieston. The Bridge of Dee is extreme left with the broad new Riverside Drive between the River Dee and the proposed villas of the suburb facing the river. More modest but still substantial houses sit to the rear. The estate of Arthurseat (the future Duthie Park) lies out of range, to the right. This is a case, not of rus in urbe but urbs in rure – the town in the country. Courtesy of Aberdeen City Libraries.*

the River Dee to the south and the new suburb of Ruthrieston and the estate of Arthurseat, which would eventually form the largest section of the Duthie Park, to the north. Thirdly he was involved in an early unsuccessful attempt to create what eventually became the Duthie Park, an undertaking hampered by a fruitless search for Arthur Williamson, the lost heir of the Arthurseat estate who had vanished in Australia (this was a few years before Miss Duthie appeared on the scene). Beattie had plans for developing Arthurseat House as a museum and aquarium, and it did later serve as a museum and tearoom within the Duthie Park. Beattie would doubtless have been further involved in the Park's planning and laying out, had not death intervened.

He died suddenly of a heart attack on 10 January 1877, while surveying at the estate of Ecclesgreig, in connection with his work as an inspector of enclosures. He was walking through a field in company with the laird, Captain Forsyth Grant, when he was struck down. Efforts by the Captain and Mrs Grant to revive him were in vain. Perhaps the Ruthrieston project had taken its toll. In addition, he had weeks earlier and possibly with some reluctance left his beloved Rubislaw Den as new plans were afoot to develop the estate.

*The Aberdeen Journal* wrote of 'those rare talents that have raised him to the top of his profession.' Another obituarist recorded, 'He had a minute and exact acquaintance with the topography of Aberdeen, Banff and Kincardineshire. His advice was much sought after by landowners and by town and county councillors alike.' Others spoke of his aptitude for hard and accurate work, his versatility, his outstanding honesty and how he treated landowners and tenants with the same courtesy. The vagueness over Beattie's year of birth dogged him till the end. His death notice stated: 'Suddenly, in the 73rd year of his age.' One obituarist noted, 'he was in his 74th year,' another, 'few would think Mr Beattie had attained the ripe age of 76.' Perhaps he had not!

Beattie had originally taken both of his sons into partnership and the firm had become JF Beattie & Sons. The elder son continued in the profession after his father's death. The younger, likely born 'down under', had made a successful return. At the time of his father's passing he was reported as being 'a large sheep farmer in Australia.'

\*\*\*

Returning to the future Union Terrace Gardens, Beattie here is handling the same terrain as is shown in the idyllic painting of 1862 (page 39), and the drab valley of the same era (page 44). His 'Sketch' was made only a few years after these illustrations appeared but is years ahead in concept, boldly emphasising the Gardens' prominence at the heart of the city, its perimeters defined by streets and by Union Bridge. At the bottom right, (partly visible) the office of the architect Archibald Simpson stands on the corner of Belmont Street and Union Street – a nice gesture, for the young James Matthews had been articled to Simpson. Continuing left is Simpson's

*Beattie's 'Sketch' of the proposed Denburn Gardens – later Union Terrace Gardens, 1869.*

magnificent Aberdeen Hotel (1817), one of the earliest buildings in Union Street.

Belmont Street, dating from the 1770s, runs between the two Simpson buildings. The buildings on the east side of the street have been deliberately omitted, giving us exceptionally fine views of the recently built Belmont Street Congregational Church and the precise delineation of the Triple Kirks complex with, from left, the West Free, the Brick Spire, the South Free and the East Free. By the end of the century, Aberdeen Trades Hall had gone up in the garden space next door to the Triple Kirks, obliterating, to howls of anguish, a view of their south elevation.

Beatie's handling of garden space is an interesting example of *rus in urbe* (an illusion of the countryside in the city) which is woven through much of the 'Sketch', with the *rus* skilfully manicured to spill into the *urbs*. His great feeling for the lie of the land is evident in the expert manner in which he worked with awkward contours. There is a feeling of room in what is a tight space, though there is little even he can do about the guddle of buildings in the rear.

The iron pedestrian footbridge is shown running from Woolmanhill – the district carried further south in these pre-Rosemount Viaduct days – to Union Terrace. When the bridge came into existence a few years later it had, as well as 'connectivity', the additional function of exclusion. It prevented further incursion from housing. It was light and graceful in appearance, yet was designed to give access to a sewerage works, obedient to the fashionable maxim that such things should be beautiful as well as useful. Similarly its east staircase, to the left of the Triple Kirks, was the model for the handsome staircases which remain one of the most notable features of the Gardens.

In Beattie's interpretation, the Gardens are shown with upper and lower terraces and also a middle section which continues on under the pedestrian bridge to form a small island-shaped upper garden, bordered by trees on either side. Continuing his *rus in urbe* theme, Beattie incorporates domestic gardens as he moves north beyond the Gardens' *pro tem* boundary. Black's Buildings (built by local wine merchant James Black in 1789) to the right and Denburn Terrace to the left, are softened by long front lawns. Just west of Black's Buildings, a little tree-lined avenue, whose gate piers have lamppost finials, leads out from the Gardens to Skene Street and to the Royal Infirmary at Woolmanhill Hospital, one of Archibald Simpson's finest works. It forms a fitting end piece for the east side of the Gardens. A small lodge beside the gate piers here matches another at the entrance to the Hospital.

On the Union Bridge/Union Terrace corner, Albert can be spotted in his chair. Union Terrace Gardens was not in existence when the Prince Consort was installed on this corner in 1863, but Beattie has skilfully incorporated the statue into a planned entrance he created for the Gardens, giving definition to both. Opposite Albert, he provides a good view of the elusive tower house, Nos 1–3 Union Terrace, which preceded the Monkey House. He marries Union Terrace with the Gardens, transforming the Corbie Heugh, which had seen better days, into a sprinkling of trees on the brae, with a thicker upper row forming one side of an avenue flanking the houses of the Terrace. We have a rare view of the depth of the Baptist Church, later Bon Accord Free, half way along. Union Terrace at this time was not open to vehicular traffic, but Beattie lends a little touch of grandeur, showing a coach heading hopefully towards Skene Terrace. At the foot of the 'Sketch', Union Bridge offers a brilliant vista, north to Woolmanhill Hospital.

Chapter Five

# HIGH SOCIETY IN UNION TERRACE

Union Terrace came into being very soon after Union Street was laid out. On 3 June 1807 the trustees for the New Streets announced that they planned to lay out a terrace some 30 to 35 feet wide, replacing the path running northward from the junction with Union Street and opposite the top of the Planted Bank, at that time the 'in' name for the Corbie Heugh (the promised 30 to 35 feet width appears not to have been implemented until 1878). Building stances on the west side of the new terrace running as far back as the grounds belonging to Mr Charles Bannerman of Crimonmogate and others would be offered (Bannerman's land included the Huntly Street/Crimon Place area). Anyone applying for a stance in 'that delightful situation' was to be accommodated on reasonable terms with 'Lots of any extent' the trustees added. Building on the east side was officially prohibited. Thus feuars were provided with excellent views of the rural scene opposite, and the new Terrace being a cul-de-sac, offered seclusion.

Old drawings and photographs of the area show tantalising glimpses of the townhouse at Nos 1–3 Union Terrace at the south-west corner with Union Street, on the site of the old Doocot. This house, occupying the best lot and certainly the most extensive one, was large, imposing and plain, but its plainness was set off by a turreted stair-block placed well-forward on the corner. Nos 1–3 looked as if it belonged to an earlier age and could have passed for an old Scots townhouse. It might have been the survivor of a sprinkling of houses near the Doocot Croft – one belonging to Alexander Innes of Breda is shown on late eighteenth-century maps – and may have been retained because it fell in with the line of the new terrace. Whatever its origins, it was acquired by Harry Lumsden of Belhelvie Lodge, laird, businessman and lawyer. No. 1 turned the corner into the Terrace from Union Street and acted as his family's winter residence, while No. 3 was his

# UNION TERRACE GARDENS

*A painting of Union Bridge and surrounding area c.1815. Extreme left, the Lumsdens' townhouse at No. 1 Union Terrace. The start of the Terrace can be seen – a narrow path. The Corbie Heugh lies below. Right of Union Bridge is the Aberdeen Hotel block, (Jamieson & Carry these days) and on the other side, of Belmont Street is Archibald's Simpson's office. The great church of St Nicholas, right. The little spire on the horizon belongs to Gordon's Hospital. Pantiled cottages of Windmill Brae huddle in the foreground.*

legal chambers and lay entirely on Union Terrace. There was a narrow gap between the turreted house and its neighbours which were uniformly plain and substantial houses in the early days, with only a little variation in height and dormer design. The gap remains.

Harry's Lumsden's wife, Kitty McVeagh, was a member of a well-known Huntly textile manufacturing family. She was a favourite of the Duchess of Gordon, Duchess Jean, a neighbour at Huntly Lodge and famed for her intelligence, *joie de vivre* and beauty. She was painted by both Reynolds and Romney. She raised the Gordon Highlanders for her husband, promising a kiss to every unwary recruit, with the King's Shilling – the recruiting payment – placed between her teeth.

This was a great era for socialising and Union Terrace, so near the Assembly Rooms, later extended to become the Music Hall, was at the heart of the social scene. 'Even though Union Street and Union Terrace were only partly built up, people were gradually moving west from their houses in the Green, Marischal Street, the Quay, Exchequer Row and other older parts of the town,' recorded Harry Lumsden's granddaughter, Louisa Lumsden, in her *Memories of Aberdeen* (1927). The autumn race meeting at the Links would be followed by an 'ordinary', an evening of dancing at the Assembly Rooms, where the supper was at a fixed price. It was virtually exclusive to the county set who had been largely responsible for funding the building of the Assembly Rooms, which, incidentally, helped to make Archibald Simpson's reputation as an architect. These evenings of dancing were something of a marriage market.

'For the first winter after their marriage,' wrote Louisa, 'my parents (Clements and Jane Lumsden) lived with the old folk (Harry and Kitty Lumsden, her grandparents), who in winter lived at No. 1 Union Terrace and in the summer at Belhelvie Lodge,' adding, 'Winters in Aberdeen were very gay.' The ladies of the Lumsden family and Mrs Peter Farquharson of Whitehouse gave balls in their Union Terrace residences, as did Lady Innes of Edengight who was round the corner in Migvie House in Silver Street, and Colonel Hay in his fine house in the Upperkirkgate. Miss Anne Davidson, a

*Clements Lumsden by James Giles RSA.*

*Jane Lumsden.*

neighbour in Union Terrace, records her continuing round of social calls on the great and the good of Town and County in her delightful *Journal* of 1844 to 1847. Anne's father, Duncan Davidson of Tillychetly and Inchmarlo, was a lawyer, her mother Frances, the daughter of Patrick Pirie, owner of Stoneywood Paper Works. As with Harry and Kitty Lumsden, gentry and wealthy manufacturers mixed and intermarried. Anne Davidson was a regular visitor at No. 1 Union Terrace, where Clements' wife Jane, daughter of a county laird, James Forbes of Echt, was an inveterate hostess. 'We called at Mrs Clements Lumsden . . .' writes Anne in her *Journal* on 7 January 1846. Or a little later, 'We went to a party at Mrs Clements Lumsden. It was rather slow at first . . .' and a few days after that, 'We had a dinner party at Mr and Mrs Clements Lumsden.' Guests included the Farquharsons of Ballogie, the Robertsons of Balgownie, Farquhar Hadden, Fred Holland and a Mr Lea. 'It went off tolerably well,' Anne wrote. The Haddens owned the great textile mills at the Green and Grandholm, the Hollands owned Broadford Works. Later, Anne recorded, 'I hear Mr Clements Lumsden is seriously ill.' But the next day, 'Mr C Lumsden is better.' Little wonder Clements sometimes took to his bed, what with the remorseless round of entertaining, his everyday legal business and representing his irate neighbours in their continuing dispute with the Town Council over the Planted Bank. It must have been a trifle embarrassing to threaten the Council with exposure in the press over their neglect of the 'Bank' one day, and to sit next to prominent councillors at one of his wife's dinner parties the next.

Clements was Harry Lumsden's eighth and youngest son. He became a lawyer like his father and was initially in partnership with his brother Henry. Later he joined forces with John Robertson, a Marischal College graduate who had served his law apprenticeship with Francis Edmond, the wealthy, redoubtable Free Kirker, and the firm became Lumsden & Robertson, advocates, or sometimes vice versa.

Just as in his father's day, Clements lived with his family at No. 1 Union Terrace, with his legal chambers at No. 3. He and Jane had several brilliant offspring. Henry, their eldest son, became a Colonel in the Royal Madras Artillery. On retirement, he made one of the earliest translations of the Anglo-Saxon epic poem *Beowulf* into English verse, perhaps an

*Rachel Lumsden.*  *Dame Louisa Lumsden.*

unexpected accomplishment for an artillery officer. Written in rhyming couplets and published in 1881 by Kegan Paul, it was a scholarly work, complete with introduction, footnotes and endnotes. James, the second son, followed in the family tradition and became a lawyer, and two daughters, Catherine and Rachel, at different periods, were honorary superintendents of the Royal Hospital for Sick Children in Aberdeen. The last and quite remarkable appointment that Rachel held, from 1885 to 1897, was at the Royal Infirmary, Woolmanhill where conditions were at rock bottom. After an unofficial approach from a senior member of the medical staff, she took over as honorary superintendent, head nurse, matron and housekeeper. She brought trained nurses from London to take over as ward sisters, instituted a three-year training scheme for local nurses – the first such in Scotland – established a superannuation fund, advised the hospital board on planning and staffing and in general did much to remove the stigma that surrounded nursing at that time and established it as a worthwhile and properly structured career for respectable young women. Her sister, Dame Louisa Innes Lumsden (1840–1935), the youngest of Clements' seven children and author of the *Memories of Aberdeen*, and an autobiography, *Yellow Leaves* (1933), was one of the leading women scholars of her day. She read Classics at Girton College Cambridge, where she was one of the first five women undergraduates and later became Classics tutor at Girton and at Cheltenham Ladies' College, and was the first headmistress of St Leonard's School, St Andrews. St Andrews University honoured her with the degree of LLD, a rare accolade for a woman at that time.

Clements died in 1853, by which time he was living at No. 17 Albyn Place, 'quite in the country,' as Louisa recalls. The following year, the family rented No. 1 Union Terrace to the Northern Club, recently established by members of the local aristocracy and county gentlemen. The legal firm of Robertson & Lumsden remained for a time at No. 3 Union Terrace, with John Robertson continuing as head of firm. In the late 1870s No. 1 was taken over by the restaurateur George Watson but a few years later the whole building was demolished. Sir Alexander Anderson, Lord Provost and businessman *extrordinaire* who lived at No. 16, had long had his eye on the site, the finest in Aberdeen.

By 1881, Anderson had acquired the whole corner site, Nos 1–3. Here he built the new Northern Assurance headquarters which were completed by 1884, three years before his death, at a cost of £40,000. The architect was A Marshall Mackenzie, James Matthews' partner and a giant in his profession. The building mirrored the confidence and aspirations of Aberdeen's business community at this time, and remains a brilliant showcase for the Victorian granite trade. Built of finely-axed Kemnay granite, the amazing detail on the façade is best viewed from across Union Street. The quadrant of Doric pillars at the entrance gave the impression of a cage and is one theory behind the origin of the nickname the 'Monkey House' – even more apt after the gates were added. The magnificent ground-floor office was divided by polished columns of Aberdeen granite, with wall panels of Californian redwood and American white walnut. There was ample accommodation available on the upper floors for 'dwelling houses for two officials.'

Moving northward along the Terrace, the Post Office Directory 1858 to 1859 shows the advocates, Davidson & Cooper, subsequently Davidson & Garden at No. 7 – the Davidsons in question being the Davidsons of

*Sir Alexander Anderson's splendid Northern Assurance Company offices, dressed overall, perhaps for the visit of Edward VII and Queen Alexandra to inaugurate the Marischal College frontage in 1906.*

Inchmarlo, the family of the diarist Anne Davidson. At the same address by the 1880s was John Willet CE, who had engineered the Denburn Valley Line in the 1860s. More of him in Chapter Eight. His son, John C Willet, advocate, who had served his apprenticeship along the road with Robertson & Lumsden, shared chambers in the same building with two other lawyers. He seems to have had a middling successful career: Secretary and Treasurer of the Aberdeen Conservative Association for example, and Clerk and Treasurer of the Banchory-Devenick School Board. However in 1895 when he was just forty, his membership of the Society of Advocates in Aberdeen was terminated. One wonders why.

Peter Cleland came to Aberdeen from Edinburgh in 1847 when he was appointed drawing master at the Mechanics' Institute, forerunner of Gray's

*The artist Peter Cleland.*

School of Art. He lived at No. 8 Union Terrace for a number of years where he also took classes. His best known work, one of great social interest, was a painting of Queen Victoria and Prince Albert arriving at Waterloo Quay on their first visit to Aberdeen in 1848, the year of revolutions throughout Europe. No revolutions here, only the great and the good of the city, bristling in formal array, waiting to greet them. Nevertheless, the Royal couple and their children might be mistaken for a well-heeled but apprehensive family of European refugees as they stand under a welcome arch with the coping stone bearing the word 'Victoria', writ large and flanked by two large white stars. Provost George Thompson to the fore on the right-hand group would have been responsible. He was chairman of the Aberdeen White Star Line, and the white star ornamentation was a subtle mode of advertising carried out by both him and his son-in-law and partner, Sir William Henderson of Devanha House whose attic pediment bears two white stars to this day. Cleland, who sketched himself in the back row of the right-hand group, was a popular teacher but decided to leave Union Terrace for Edinburgh after twenty years in Aberdeen.

*Cleland's painting of the arrival of Queen Victoria and family at Waterloo Quay in 1848.*

Another legal firm, Chalmers & Farquhar, was at No. 14. Of one of the partners, James Chalmers, it was said, 'He was popular with the farming community, and to whatever enterprise he gave his support, he gave it wholly and heartedly.' As Messrs C & PH Chalmers the firm became one of the best-known in Aberdeen. But Union Terrace was not peopled entirely by lawyers. A diversity of professional firms and distinguished citizens was to be found in the Terrace throughout the nineteenth century, drawn by first the location, both prestigious and convenient, and later the view of the developing Gardens below.

Moving along towards the centre of the Terrace, the third block from the Monkey House, Nos 10–13, were tall, plain buildings, with rounded doors occupied in 1891–1899 according to the Post Office Directory by, respectively, a surgeon, George Edmund; the factor of the Cluny estates Ranald R MacDonald; a chartered accountant, James Tytler and C & P H Chalmers, advocates. One of these buildings offered temporary lodgings to homeless sailors. This group of buildings became the Grand Hotel, later the Caledonian, which retained the original rounded doors, and in more recent

# UNION TERRACE GARDENS

*GNSR's plan for a railway station beside Union Terrace Gardens in 1890. A path beside Prince Albert's sedentary statue leads down to the Gardens where a few walks have been laid out. The balustrades have not yet appeared. The tall houses with round-headed doors third along from the Northern Assurance offices, extreme left, were transformed into the Grand later the Caledonian Hotel. The triangular building to the right was Bon Accord Free Church, where the Old County Buildings were later built. The GNSR station never materialised, possibly due to lack of cash or change in plan.*

times the Caledonian Thistle. Its story is intriguing. The entry for A Marshall Mackenzie in the 'Directory of Scottish Architects' Biography Report' shows that in 1891 he carried out 'additions' to the Grand Hotel in Union Terrace or 'Mann's Grand' as its owner liked it to be called. This is the first mention of the Hotel in the Directory, and it would appear that Mackenzie had not built it from scratch, but carried out a very superior makeover of the Union Terrace townhouses. The Aberdeen Town Council Minutes of October 1891 makes references to new sewers and also to extending back to Diamond Street. This does not indicate a new building, rather these 'additions' noted in the Directory. Mackenzie would have added an ornate façade, a handsome flight of steps at the entrance, elaborate plasterwork and he would have gone up a storey and a half, as he already had done elsewhere. The hotel stands on the same site as Nos 10–13, and is listed in the Post Office Directory of 1892–1893 issue as Mann's Palace Hotel (a quick revision of the previous entry for 1891–1892) whose residents were now displaced. Several found new accommodation nearby while C & PH Chalmers, Advocates went to Golden Square where they remained for many years. No. 13 became the Aberdeen University Club for a time.

This is a tangled tale of two hotels which really begins at the famous Palace Hotel, which stood at the junction of Union Street and the new Bridge Street and was built for Pratt & Keith, drapers and silk mercers in 1873. Pratt & Keith operated on the ground floor, Lorimer's boot and shoe business and other smaller shops occupied the lower regions and the upper floors were leased to Mr Charles Mann where for many years he operated the luxury Palace Hotel, which like Union Terrace offered fine views over the Gardens. In 1891, after John Keith's death, the Great North of Scotland Railway (GNSR) acquired the Palace and embarked on a programme of refurbishment which included the addition of a further storey. Charles Mann was not retained by the new regime. He must have been very bitter at this turn of events, which explained his decision to open a new hotel as near as possible to the Palace and even to call it the Palace, with the aim of

*A spectacular postcard of Mann's Grand Hotel. Note the arches in Union Terrace Gardens, and the statue of Robert Burns. He is not wearing the kilt, though his heavily pleated frock coat gives that impression. The date 1891 is spurious. The plinth is inscribed 'Burns', nothing else. Perhaps Charles Mann added it for the photograph, to tie in with the date the hotel opened. The tunnel linking it with the Gardens may date from around this period. Courtesy of Aberdeen City Libraries.*

*An early view of Union Terrace showing Mann's Grand, extreme right. The original Palace Hotel stands on Union Street extreme left.*

putting the original Palace out of business. Hence the speedy conversion of the Union Terrace townhouses. The GNSR took him to court over his use of the name 'Palace' for his new hotel, arguing that under the terms of their purchase they were entitled to keep that name for the original building. The court found for the railway company so Mann was obliged to rename his new hotel 'The Grand'.

Moving on, No. 15 was the home of James Blaikie of Blaikie Bros, iron founders, whose nameplate used to be seen on many railway bridges throughout the North-east. Aberdeen Chamber of Commerce moved into this building around 1915 and perhaps it was they who had a particularly fine door case inserted into the original opening. Next door at No. 16 was Robert Dyce MD, Lecturer in Midwifery at Marischal College, and brother of the famous artist William Dyce who painted the murals of the robing room of the House of Lords and much else. Sir Alexander Anderson later lived at No. 16 for a time, as already noted. Nos 15 and 16 are both early nineteenth century. No. 19 was the handy manse of the Rev. Charles Ross, minister of Bon Accord Church which was to be found a little further along Union Terrace. Lewis Smith the bookseller was at No. 20 and John Lyell the gunmaker at No. 21. Later residents included the factor Ranald R Macdonald at No. 16, decanted from what became 'Mann's Grand' and Brown & Watt, architects at No. 17. One of George Watt's finest works in 1891, where he prevailed in a strongly contested competition, was the Free Library, to give its initial title, later the Public Library in Rosemount Viaduct, for which his firm was well-placed. The *Bon Accord Press* office, William Smith proprietor and editor, was at No. 18, one of the early addresses of that popular weekly paper which survived until 1959, though by then 'much altered.' It was delightfully satirical in its early days. There was also a good sprinkling of doctors, dentists and accountants much of the way along the Terrace, even a vet and a shoer of horses with Mr William Fraser, surgeon, bringing up the rear at No. 31, convenient for the Royal Infirmary at Woolmanhill. We are now moving towards the Skene Street end where townhouses peter out, to be replaced by tenements in the Aberdeen vernacular. These were the homes or the lodgings of the superior working classes: milliner, sick-nurse, shuttle maker, dressmaker, grocer, provision dealer, confectioner and druggist.

Union Terrace had the merit of offering pleasant views, first across to the Corbie Heugh under its various names, but in the later years of the nineteenth century it underwent marked changes, becoming part of the new access to Rosemount when the cul-de-sac at Skene Terrace was removed in 1884. Some of the older buildings, plain but dignified, began to be replaced by newer, more fashionable ones. Beside Diamond Place and north of it are further magnificent Renaissance-style buildings, the 'palazzi', but these will be tackled when we look at Rosemount Viaduct which has a close relationship with the north end of the Valley and of the Terrace. But there is an earlier history of a building towards the end of the Terrace, a roughly triangular-shaped kirk which started life in 1823 as the Union Terrace Baptist Chapel. 'Baptist Chapel Union Terrace is in the course of being built, measures 60 by 50 feet. Mr John Gilmour is minister.' So Robert Wilson reported in his *Delineation of Aberdeen* of 1822. One of the city's early Baptist groups had formed a congregation and feued a site and 'Mr (John) Smith was employed as architect.' By 1827, the Baptists had received an offer they couldn't refuse and moved to John Street where they built a new chapel.

The buildings were acquired by a breakaway congregation from Trinity Church, and became Bon Accord Church. This congregation called a

*Bon Accord Old Free Kirk, Union Terrace.*

minister of their own choosing the Rev. Gavin Parker, a name to be reckoned with. In the summer of 1843 his flock came solidly 'out' at the Disruption of the Church of Scotland, and Parker preached in the open in Union Terrace on Sunday mornings and in a Skene Terrace church in the evenings. George Bain, a Gilcomston weaver, and the father of Professor Alexander Bain was a leading member of the congregation here. The kirk was eventually rouped at the upset price to a member, Dr John Campbell, who bought it on behalf of the congregation and it became the new Bon Accord Free Church. In 1896, the congregation moved to an impressive suite of church buildings in the new Rosemount Viaduct where they remain to this day.

*\*\*\**

**Sir Alexander Anderson 1802-1887**
**One of the greatest Aberdonians**
Sir Alexander Anderson, advocate in Aberdeen, was born in Strichen, Aberdeenshire, a son of the manse. He was a Marischal College graduate

Sir Alexander Anderson.

and senior partner of Adam and Anderson, advocates (ie solicitors in Aberdeen) from 1830 to 1866, the best-known Aberdeen law firm in its day. The local historian Dr Alexander Keith, described Anderson as the man who single-handedly 'projected Aberdeen into the modern age,' and as 'one of the greatest heads of Bon Accord.' Anderson also successfully survived the occasional financial scrape.

During an outstanding career which touched so much of Aberdeen business life, Sir Alexander promoted the Aberdeen Fire and Life Assurance in 1836 which evolved into the Northern Assurance Company whose magnificent head office at No. 1 Union Terrace (the Monkey House) remains one of Aberdeen's great granite showpieces, replaced the turreted house. The North of Scotland Bank, the Aberdeen Market Co., a number of Railway Companies, a gas undertaking, the Cairnton Water Scheme, and the City of Aberdeen Land Association which purchased the Lands of Torry and Rubislaw and later evolved into CALA, were all Sir Alexander's creations. As well as the Northern Assurance Co.'s head office, several other of his ventures begat fine buildings, the headquarters of the North of Scotland Bank in Castle Street (1840–1842) for example, and the Aberdeen Market Co.'s New Market building in 1842 both by Archibald Simpson. The latter was demolished regardless of considerable anger in 1971. He pressed successfully for the creation of the new Grammar School in Skene Street, and for a new Townhouse. 'Disputes clustered round Anderson's head like bees round a honey pot,' wrote Alex Keith, 'and he seemed to thrive on them.'

Chapter Six

# VIADUCTS, BALUSTRADES AND OTHER THINGS

Union Terrace Gardens and Rosemount Viaduct were the brainchildren of the visionary architect James Matthews. The first phase of these improvements, the creation of about 80 per cent of Union Terrace Gardens, had been carried out in the late 1870s. Matthews had already left the Council after his first stint, but his stamp was on it. The next phase, which would also see the completion of Union Terrace Gardens, would be 'a New Street from the Denburn Valley to Rosemount' made possible under the Aberdeen Extension and Improvement of 1883. In 1893 the historian William Robbie wrote in retrospect:

> Long after Rosemount had become a populous district it continued at a great disadvantage through the want of a proper access from the centre of the city . . . It was clear to everybody that the most convenient access was by throwing a series of arches across the Denburn to the line of Mount Street, but equally evident that the expense of this route would be a serious matter. The Town Council however resolved to face it in a liberal spirit, and though it involved heavy expenditure plans were sanctioned that resulted in Rosemount Viaduct which is one of the greatest improvements effected in recent years.

The events leading up to this development had caused much interest, even controversy in the city. There had been Improvement and anti-Improvement sections within the Town Council of 1882, and a special election was held to put the choice to the electorate. The Improvers were returned with a large majority with James Matthews back at the helm, now as Lord Provost. His clear and elegant signature approving Council minutes was reassuring, his early exhortation to his fellow councillors to get on with things, to 'prioritise' as we would say today, boded well.

The building of Rosemount Viaduct was planned in two sections. The Council lost little time in going ahead with the upper section, which was completed by 1885 and ran from the north end of Union Terrace, breaking through Skene Street, to the foot of South Mount Street. The shorter section remained to be tackled. It had been planned first, but was, if anything, more difficult than the upper section as it involved demolitions – this was a populous area – and the spanning of the Lower Denburn Valley, including crossing the railway line.

With the upper section accomplished, the Town Council elected to purchase various properties in the lower section with a view to demolition, clearing the way for action. And so, with much already achieved, Matthews, on the expiry of his term as Lord Provost in 1886, gave notice of motion that the construction of the lower section of the new access should now go ahead. The starting point was the end of Schoolhill, beside the Triple Kirks at their junction with Belmont Street, then straight on to link with the upper section at the north end of Union Terrace.

The design for the lower section was open to competition and plans by both the city surveyor, William Boulton, and an 'outside Engineer', George Herd CE, were submitted to the Improvements Committee – Councillor John Morgan, master mason, Bailie Rust, granite merchant and the incredibly

*William Boulton, city surveyor.*

active Sir Alexander Lyon, the George Street hide and tallow merchant who was much involved in the laying out of Union Terrace Gardens among other, later parks. Boulton's design was chosen though Herd had given him a run for his money. He received an honorarium. At £9,750 Boulton's design was cheaper, it had the better appearance, it provided 'a fitting termination to the north end of Union Terrace Gardens' and it offered a larger area of ground available for feuing. The watchword in those days was not 'How much can we borrow?' but 'How much can we save?' The principal feature of Boulton's plans was the building of the magnificent Denburn Viaduct which would carry the proposed new road by three arches, above, respectively, the Denburn Road, the railway, with the Denburn in culvert – this is the Lower Denburn Valley – and the north end of Union Terrace Gardens, where at time of writing, the wheelchair entrance is located.

Boulton was determined that only the whitest of white and the darkest of blue granite would be used for the bridge which he selected personally, the former from Mr Fyfe's Kemnay quarry, the latter from Messrs Manuelle's quarry at Dyce. Deep pink Correnie granite was chosen for the panels sunk in the pilasters that were interspersed among the balusters. This colour scheme, as close to red, white and blue as granite can get, may have been a belated tribute to Queen Victoria's Golden Jubilee of 1887. Work began in May 1888. There had been some delay, for the managers of the GNSR had, perhaps a trifle late in the day, seen the advantage of building a suburban station on the Denburn Viaduct and started discussions with the Town Council, who gave the idea a cautious welcome. Quid pro quos came into force. The Council insisted that the masonry of the new Schoolhill Station should be similar in quality and colour to the Viaduct and to accommodate the railway they agreed to make the three spans of the Viaduct measure respectively 25, 40 and 25 feet instead of three 30-feet arches. Ground to the east and west of the railway line was sold to allow the building of Schoolhill Station.

The Viaduct was completed with considerable speed in spite of the difficulties that were incurred through building the arches on skew (slanting), and work on Schoolhill Station was able to begin in the autumn of 1890. It opened in September 1893 with all trains running between

*A job well done. The Denburn Viaduct has been built. Bowler hats, masons, journeymen and apprentices pose for a photograph.*

Aberdeen and Dyce calling there. A two-storey building, approached by a walkway of decking, with waiting rooms at platform level, a booking hall on the second floor, and with a three-storey tower, it was popular with pupils coming to school from the country and was particularly handy for Robert Gordon's pupils and theatre-goers. It was the ideal stop to unload scenery for His Majesty's Theatre. After closure, the station became a tearoom and was eventually demolished in February 1975. It was a shabby building by the end but, with hindsight, had it been restored as a unique tower building on the Denburn Viaduct, it could have been put to a number of uses, including a café linked to H M Theatre, a railway museum or both, and more.

These Victorians took enormous pains with the Denburn Viaduct. Today we are scarcely aware of its existence as we walk or drive over it travelling from Schoolhill towards the Theatre or Library or vice versa. But look up as you are driving towards it on the southbound side of the Denburn dual carriageway, or looking across from the east end of Union Bridge and appreciate a virtually unknown Aberdeen gem.

Demolition went ahead. The remnant of Mutton Brae, which had already lost its lower houses during the building of the Denburn Valley Railway in 1865–1867, was swept away. The weavers had gone years before, but the surviving little community of pawnbrokers and chimney sweeps had to find new homes. Several went to Windy Wynd, the westerly half of Spring Garden where there was already a small colony. With the houses gone, the Denburn Viaduct appeared to pass perilously close to the Triple Kirks. It cut in front of Black's Buildings, causing them to acquire an awkward look, as if they had been carelessly deposited there. Within the curtilage of Union Terrace Gardens, Denburn Terrace was pulled down and its inhabitants dispersed: James Reith, grocer, to Craigie Street; John Donald, hatter, to Argyll Place and Alex Duffton, china merchant, to King Street. James Stephen, gilder and framemaker went to nearby Woolmanhill where his shop remained till the end. With the bridge built and the railway line crossed, the Rosemount Viaduct could then continue to its goal at the end of Union Terrace via what had become an interesting embankment. Boulton created a retaining wall which was to form the new northern end of Union Terrace Gardens. With economy in mind – he was a man of talent in his profession, but one whose watchword was 'thrift' – he used the down-takings from Denburn Terrace and other rubble to build up this newly created northern end as an amphitheatre.

The embankment was carried round from the westerly arch of the Denburn Viaduct by an easy curve to Union Terrace. On the line of this curve, a slip road was formed to serve as a more direct access to Union Street and the Railway Station. 'The slope of this curved position,' said the Council Minutes, 'to be laid out in an ornamental manner so as to form a continuation of Union Terrace Gardens' – the 'triangular' piece of the Gardens at pavement level. The statue of Sir William Wallace would take up its position beside the newly created 'triangle,' even before it was planted out. Meanwhile, the newly constructed section of embankment almost opposite Union Terrace Gardens became available for building on, offering that 'larger area of ground available for feuing' as Boulton had

# UNION TERRACE GARDENS

*The 'slip' road lies between the north end of Union Terrace Gardens, right, and the 'triangle' addition at street level, with Prince Albert, left, and Wallace, right.*

*Wallace welcomes us to the completed lower section of Rosemount Viaduct, with, from left, Education Salvation and Damnation all in place. The statue preceded them all.*

*A. Marshall Mackenzie, Architect* par excellence.

prophesied. First there came the Public Library, designed by George Watt in Renaissance style in 1891, then the South Free Kirk in 1892 with its massive Corinthian portico and dome above, almost a civic building with ecclesiastical undertones, reminiscent of Simpson's lost university. The architect was Matthews' partner, Alexander Marshall Mackenzie. In the genesis of both buildings the largesse of John Gray, ironfounder, played a large part. Finally, His Majesty's Theatre designed by Frank Matcham, theatre architect *par excellence*, and built between 1904 and 1906, was and remains a magnificent backdrop for Union Terrace Gardens.

With the building of this lower section of Rosemount Viaduct, the light iron footbridge that had linked Mutton Brae/Belmont Street and Union Terrace since 1877 was now redundant. It was scarcely fifteen years old. It was resurrected in the Duthie Park, between the upper (duck) pond and the lower pond, in a suitably truncated form where it can be seen to this day. Surplus parts were economically put to good use. A small section of its parapet remained behind, for many years, at the boundary wall of the old Albion and St Paul's side of the Triple Kirks, while a length of it was erected

# UNION TERRACE GARDENS

*The light iron footbridge was taken to the Duthie Park which opened in 1881.*

*A section from the parapet of the light iron bridge at the boundary wall of Albion and St Paul's at the Triple Kirks.*

# VIADUCTS, BALUSTRADES AND OTHER THINGS

as a railing between Woolmanhill and the Denburn Road, prior to dualling. Economy was all.

'The crowning part of these improvements,' wrote William Robbie, 'was the widening of Union Terrace by about 10 feet or 12,' which was accomplished by the erection of a series of arches along the west side of the Gardens. 'These arches answer the double purpose of a pavement for the Terrace and, in the Gardens, an agreeable shelter from the sun or from the rain,' he added. They had grown from the original three.

Additional balustrades could now be introduced. The handsome, open balustrades, all hand-carved, had been a distinctive feature of Union Bridge until it was widened between 1905 and 1908. They were not included in the new design. However, when the north section of Union Terrace Gardens and the Denburn Viaduct were being built from 1886 to 1903, these original balusters were still in place, and inspired their use on the Denburn Viaduct, the only difference being that the new additions were machine-

*An excellent view from the early 1890s of hand-tooled balusters on Union Bridge, the Gardens with the arches, and Rosemount Viaduct without His Majesty's Theatre. Some original tenements can be made out at the end of Union Terrace as the 'palazzi' are not yet complete.*

turned. Following the widening of Union Terrace, William Dyack, William Boulton's assistant, drew up a scheme for introducing granite balustrades, over a quarter of a mile of them, starting from the Denburn Viaduct thus defining the northern boundary of the Gardens and so along entire length of the Terrace, to match up with Union Bridge. The Gardens were given an appropriate finish.

On Union Terrace and Rosemount Viaduct architects took up balustrading to echo that of the Gardens with great enthusiasm. In 1891 Marshall Mackenzie had given the townhouses at Nos 10–13 Union Terrace a substantial 'makeover' to become Charles Mann's Grand Hotel. The new frontage was embellished with balusters, in tune with the originals across the road. This was perhaps the earliest manifestation of balustrading outwith Union Terrace Gardens, along with those ornamenting George Watt's handsome Public Library also of 1891, and Marshall Mackenzie's new South Free on the new embankment.

Union Terrace Gardens had been closed during work on the Viaduct and the amphitheatre. In March 1893 it was once more thrown open to the public.

We can stay in Union Terrace, picking up again from Chapter Five at Diamond Place, whose steepness, incidentally, reflects the natural slope of the Denburn Valley. That little side street ought to remind us that massive excavations were necessary, not only to erect the buildings in the Terrace but to improve and widen the carriageway and to lay out the Gardens. Though the north end of Union Terrace was originally filled with tenements, some with shops on the ground floor, the creation of Rosemount Viaduct induced a late, but brilliant transformation of the Terrace from cul-de-sac to boulevard. As Union Terrace nears the junction with Rosemount Viaduct, elaborate Italian Renaissance-style buildings have intermingled with tenements in the vernacular since the late nineteenth century. In fact several of the tenements had to make way for these Renaissance-style 'palazzi'. One such was replaced by No. 19, the architect William Kelly's superb head office for the Aberdeen Savings Bank (ASB) and his finest work, built in 1895. His meticulous craftsmanship and attention to detail rivalled that of Charles Rennie Mackintosh. The narrow frontage was

*Kelly's finest work: the headquarters of Aberdeen Savings Bank.*

imaginatively ornamented with a small balustraded balcony supported by sizeable consoles all but dominating the ornate door, while the upper balcony above was partly balustraded. ASB subsequently became a TSB, which in turn was acquired by Lloyds Bank in 1995 to become Lloyds TSB Scotland. Since this amalgamation, Kelly's wonderful bank is surplus to needs or at least, it is not required for welcoming and attending to customers. It quietly moulders on the Union Terrace–Diamond Place corner, the great iron gates locked and partly hidden by a row of wheelie bins.

We left Bon Accord Free Church in 1896 moving to a new suite of buildings on the upper section of the new Rosemount Viaduct. To finance the move, the church sold its buildings on Union Terrace. These were replaced by a group of 'palazzi', all north of Diamond Place, but all taking their cue from the style of Kelly's Savings Bank. No. 20 was built for the Aberdeen Parish Council and No. 22 was built for the Aberdeen School Board, both by Marshall Mackenzie, around 1897. Guests enjoyed a splendid ceremony at the laying of the foundation stone of No. 20. The Lord Provost proposed the health of Parish Council and a banquet at Mann's Grand followed, including salmon, turbot, roast beef, braised chicken, roast lamb and roast duckling followed by strawberry ice cream.

In 1938 Nos 20 and 22, where the balustrades continue aloft, were sold to Aberdeen County Council for over £20,000 and became known informally as the Old County Buildings. No. 25, was the work of the architectural firm of AG Sydney Mitchell and Wilson in 1902 for the Scottish Life Assurance Co. In the thirties, some if not all of the architectural family of Allans, Joseph and JAO Allan, who was also a structural engineer, had premises there.

After No. 25 came the original dwellings at the north end of Union Terrace, the plain tenements, though they had palatial No. 40 and No. 42 in their midst. No. 40, somewhat over-egged and now with a damaged doorway, was built by Sutherland & Pirie for the Scottish Legal Life Assurance Society in 1902. In the early days they shared the premises with a solicitor, a tailor and a 'teeth specialist'. The amazing No. 42, a building similar in style to No. 40, is at the very end of the row, near the corner with Skene Terrace and Rosemount Viaduct. For some time it was the headquarters

# VIADUCTS, BALUSTRADES AND OTHER THINGS

*Nos 20-22 Union Terrace: the Old County Buildings. They are now one unit.*

*No. 25 Union Terrace.*

*No. 40 Union Terrace. An early example of curved glass. The handsome doorway has been ruined.*

of James R Donald's empires: Aberdeen Picture Palaces and Aberdeen Cinemas. It had spacious rooms where rehearsals for the annual pantomime staged across at His Majesty's Theatre were held. For those who did not wish to be seen leaving, there was said to be a passage which would take you through the building and out at the Donald-owned Cinema House round in Skene Terrace. The original tenement buildings interspersed between these palazzi underwent a major restoration in the 1980s and their emergence as attractive city dwellings is still evident. Several of these buildings have shops on the ground floor – modest, but with a style of their own. No. 27 was a tobacconist; No. 29 was Herd's Lugano Café which was pleasant to drop into on one's way back from the Library; No. 30 was Smith's newsagent and confectioner, then came the Soda Fountain. I think the proprietor, Mr Berni, also owned the ice-cream shop in Crown Street.

The sharp-eyed may spot a blue and white notice, 'Stamps', affixed beside the hairdressing salon at No. 39. The Grampian Stamp Shop is, in fact at

*The palazzo and the modernised tenement flats, with the well-remembered shops below, at the north end of Union Terrace. Herd's Lugano café and its neighbour to the left became Pavarotti's.*

No. 38 and as a child I was always fascinated by a small display of stamps in the front window. This is a philatelic corner because the Aberdeen and North of Scotland Philatelic Society used to be based nearby.

No. 41, a kilt-hire shop these days, had originally been a confectioner's, owned for many years by John Mitchell. No. 44 which rounds the corner to Skene Terrace was a 'Wilburn', belonging to William Watt Hepburn's extensive grocery chain in Aberdeen. In the post-war years it became a branch of Lombard's Banking for a time. Herd's Lugano was the best known of that group, but closed down in the early 1980s. The then owner, Eric Sutherland, found several factors weighing against business: the departure of Aberdeenshire Council staff from their neighbouring palazzo after regionalisation, Alexander's buses no longer using the Wallace statue as their terminus and H M Theatre closing for renovation. That part of the Terrace was no longer the same without Herd's. But then it became Pavarotti's.

After Mr Sutherland's departure, the former Herd's Lugano and its neighbour (Nos 27–29) were taken over by a bunch of gangsters, the La Torre family, who ran the Naples-based mafia-style Camorra. The La Torres did their global homework and picked Aberdeen, with no serious organised crime and a booming oil industry, as the ideal base to launder money acquired through extortion, drug-trafficking and racketeering (I could envisage a *Scotland the What?* sketch featuring a mix-up between Torre and Torry). Antonio La Torre the third son of the family and the financial brains of the organisation, came to Aberdeen in 1984 where he established himself as a restaurateur, opening Pavarotti's – which gained a good reputation for its seafood – at the old Lugano café and its neighbour. The laundering went ahead involving numerous business transactions including buying land in Aberdeen. Justice eventually caught up with Antonio and he was arrested in Aberdeen in March 2005 and was imprisoned in Italy after trial. An Italian judge has stated that there is now no trace of the La Torre clan in Scotland, though conversely, a *Scotsman* headline of August 2014 reported that the Mafia 'tightens its grip in Aberdeen.' The La Torres were first exposed in the book *Gomorrah* by the vigilante journalist Roberto Saviano, published in Italian in 2006 and translated into English the following year. It has been

*Rounding the corner to Skene Terrace and Rosemount Viaduct. The 'Stamps' notice for the sharp-eyed is to the left.*

made into a film and is serialised on television. Nos 27–29 is still a seafood bar though with nothing to do with the La Torres, and Carmine's popular pizza restaurant is nearby.

*Robert Burns by Henry Bain Smith (1859–1896).*

CHAPTER SEVEN

# THE VERY PLACE FOR STATUES

### Albert, Prince Consort, at the junction of Union Street and Union Terrace, 1863

On 13 October 1863 a grand occasion of mixed success took place when Queen Victoria came from Balmoral to Aberdeen to inaugurate the statue of her late husband, Albert, the Prince Consort, who had died in 1861. The site chosen for the statue was the junction of Union Street and Union Terrace where the King Edward VII group of memorial statuary now stands. The rooms of No. 1 Union Terrace, the turreted house directly opposite, at that time tenanted by the Northern Club, were put at the disposal of the Queen. A temporary platform was erected to ensure that the Royal Party – the Queen, four daughters and their ladies-in-waiting – had the best possible sight of the unveiling ceremony. Perhaps to allow maximum viewing from the platform Albert was placed, a trifle uncomfortably, near the edge of the wide pavement, where he remained until overtaken by Nemesis in the form of his son. 'Unfortunately,' recorded the journalist William Carnie in his second volume of *Reporting Reminiscences*, 'the day was as bad as it could be, mist, flying showers, and downpours of rain prevailing throughout. Notwithstanding this, the crowd of onlookers was immense.'

Before the unveiling, the Rev. Professor Campbell, Principal of Aberdeen University (King's and Marischal Colleges had united at last, in 1860) 'engaged in a fervent prayer,' recalls Carnie, 'recorded by some pencillers to have occupied five minutes, by others, three times that period.' Albert, when his voluminous wrappings were eventually unfurled by 'three smart fellows of HM warship *Winchester*,' came as a shock. A tall, elegant man in life, he had been portrayed by the sculptor as what seemed to be a small man in the clutches of a large Gothic chair. The word 'statue' comes from

*Prince Albert at his original site. A fine view of Union Terrace with a miscellany of transport.*

the Latin *statuere*, to cause to stand, but this was more of a 'Sit-ye-doon, Prince Albert.' By placing Albert on what looked very like a throne, the sculptor Baron Carlo Marochetti was endowing him in death with equal status to the Queen. The sculptor's intended compliment appeared to have misfired. Her Majesty gazed at it anxiously from several viewpoints, then courteously acknowledging the people, retired, and was soon on her way back to Balmoral. 'What a lot of grumbling and disappointment found vent,' continued Carnie. 'The statue was felt to be a failure!' But far from being dropped from Royal favour, Baron Marochetti was commissioned to make an equestrian statue of Prince Albert for George Square in Glasgow.

The occasion had been a good one for Aberdeen's great opportunist provost, Alexander Anderson, or Sir Alexander as he had become when he knelt down in the billiard room of the Northern Club, which had been tricked out with bunting for the Queen's visit. At a public meeting in Aberdeen soon after Albert's death it was Provost Anderson who pushed for the erection of a statue and ascertained that the sculptor, Baron Marochetti, was in favour at court. The Italian-born aristocrat, a suave charmer and a great favourite with European Royalty, had fled to London in 1848, the year of revolutions, with the deposed French king, Louis Philippe, and quickly made his mark with the best people. It was Provost Anderson who carried off a great coup in persuading the Queen, the Widow of Windsor as she was called at this time, to come out of her self-imposed purdah and carry out her first public engagement since her husband's death. The site, beside what became the entrance to the Union Terrace Gardens, is nowadays acknowledged as the finest in the city. Not so in 1863 when the Gardens did not yet exist and when Union Terrace was still a narrow cul-de-sac. It was Anderson who foresaw that the corner had a future.

The Aberdeen statue was certainly among the earliest, if not the very first, of the Consort and was followed by an avalanche of Albert statues, many of them equestrian. But when the London Albert Memorial was mooted in 1862, Victoria returned to the Aberdeen example and gave instructions for a sedentary Albert to be sculpted, again by Marochetti. She could not have been disappointed with his Aberdeen effort after all. Sir George Gilbert Scott, designer of the Memorial, found fault with Marochetti's new sculpture, but the Baron died before he had time to make alterations, and the revised version was sculpted by others. During the Memorial's restoration in 1998, the hatless prince, still sedentary, was covered in gold leaf and, with one foot placed meaningfully on a footstool, looks ready for action.

**Sir William Wallace, The Rosemount Viaduct Triangle, 1888**
In June 1888, William Grant Stevenson's colossal bronze statue of Sir William Wallace, Guardian of Scotland, was sited on a high plinth of roughly-hewn pink granite just outside the new Rosemount Viaduct triangle, the addition to Union Terrace Gardens at street level, created by the slip road. Born in Ratho near Edinburgh in 1849, Grant Stevenson, painter and sculptor, had won an open competition to create a statue of Wallace, initiated by the patriotic Mr John Steill of Edinburgh in which twenty-five sculptors from Scotland, England, France and Italy had taken part.

There was a problem with Wallace however, which dragged on for years. Steill, of North-east parentage, a lawyer and landowner with an interest in recondite points of Scottish history, had died in 1871 leaving a bequest of

£3,000 to execute the sculpture. He gave specific details on how the work was to be carried out, the type of site to be acquired, and the precise moment in history that was represented. This was a time of heightened discussion about British interests versus 'Separatists', and the city of Edinburgh to which the statue was offered declined, in the circumstances, to find a site for something that might prove inflammatory.

Aberdeen was next on the list and much correspondence between the city's Town Council and Steill's trustees ensued. The problem now was not so much political but to find a site that corresponded with Steill's wish for prominence. This magnificent work, some 30 feet high, the most heroic statue of the Guardian in existence, was not easy to place. It was originally intended for the Castlegate, but that proved unsuitable as did the Union Terrace area. It was too large and heavy for the pavements. Borings taken in the Gardens in 1880 had shown the terrain to be unsuitable. It would not do to have a subsiding Wallace! By 1883 the Town Council agreed, with some reluctance, that the statue would be placed on top of the Mound in the new Duthie Park. Luckily there were more delays, and before Wallace could be bedded in there, the building up of the lower section of Rosemount Viaduct was approaching completion and a new and, as it proved, ideal site was created by the triangle formed by the slip road. As the Improvements Committee recorded in 1887:

> We were much impressed with the advantages which this site possesses over that in the Duthie Park, not the least important of these being its commanding character, overlooking the Denburn Valley, while its central position could not fail to render the Statue an object of much greater interest to the citizens as well as visitors to Aberdeen.

The Marquis of Lorne, Queen Victoria's son-in-law performed the unveiling ceremony and made an inappropriate speech 'of inordinate length' hailing Wallace as a symbol of imperial prowess. The Town Council, delighted at the turn of events, heaved a sigh of relief. It should be noted, incidentally, that Wallace is not placed on the grass of the triangle but on the hard pavement just outside it.

# THE VERY PLACE FOR STATUES

*Wallace and St Marks.*

*Wallace and the dome of His Majesty's Theatre.*

*Wallace supervising the building of His Majesty's.*

*Wallace takes centre stage.*

The attention to the details of Wallace's garb and gear is superb. 'The pose of the figure is sternly erect and the features are those of a man born to be a leader,' so wrote William Robbie. 'His great two-handed sword rests in his right hand while his outstretched left arm indicates that he is directing the English friars sent to negotiate a peace treaty with him: "Go back to your masters and tell them that we came not here to treat, but to fight and set Scotland free".' This was 'the precise moment in history' that Steill had hoped to catch. That, and the other inscriptions round the base, give a feeling for Wallace's cause and make stimulating reading. This is a statue that is also a book. Now every August, an annual commemoration for Wallace is held round the statue with a reading of the Declaration of Arbroath, wreath laying, pageants, songs of freedom and lament, bagpipes, prayers, and a march-past.

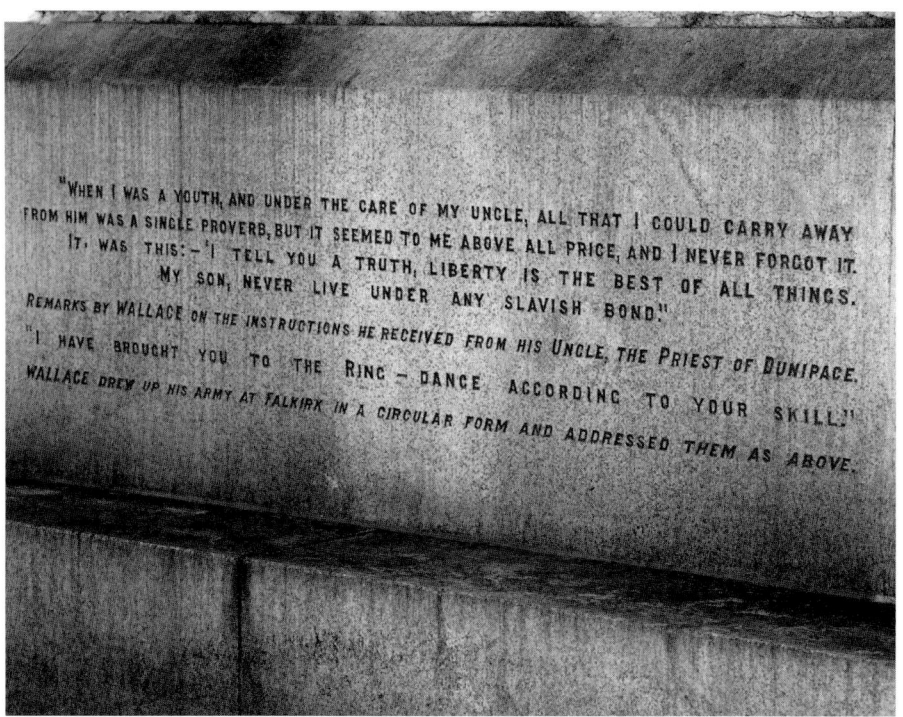

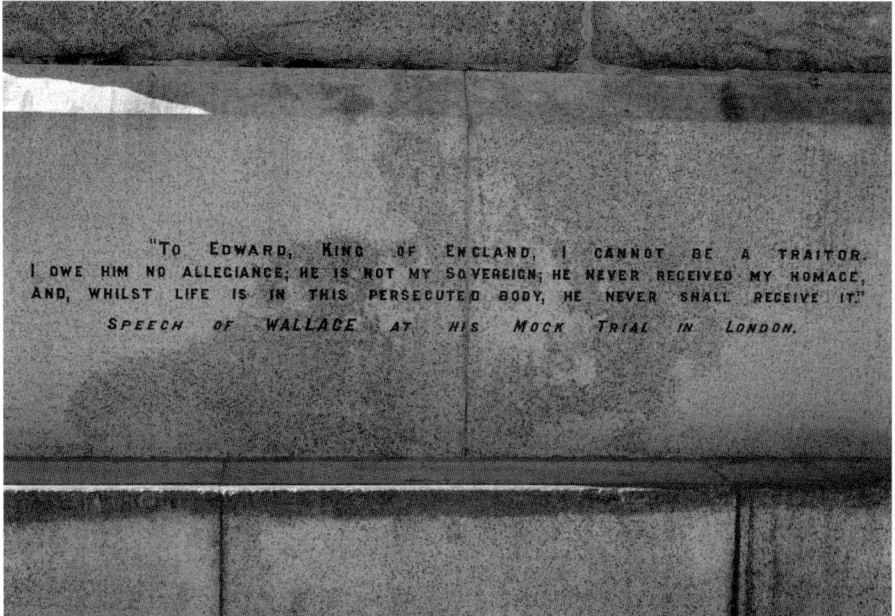

*The Wallace Statue is also a book.*

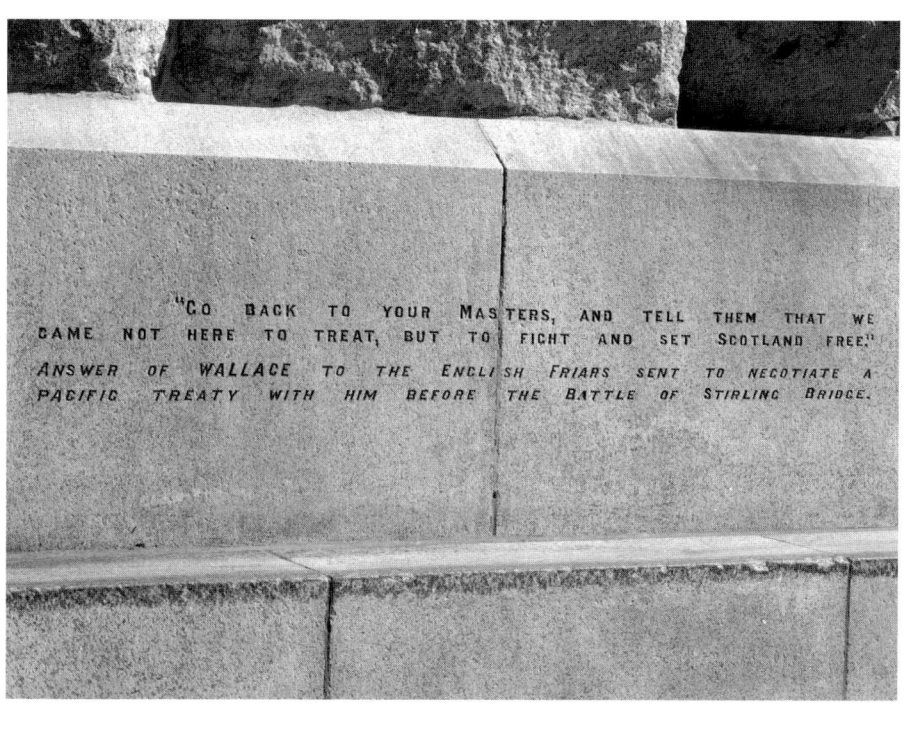

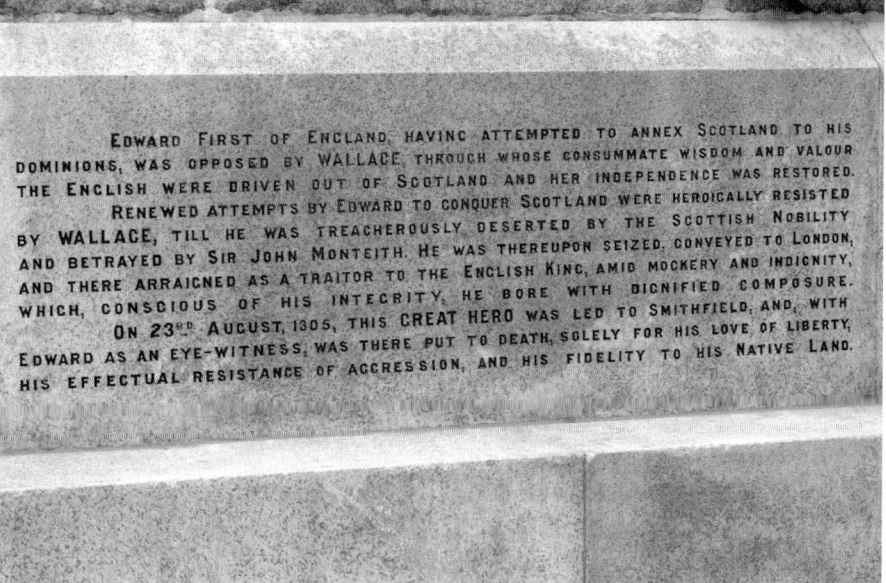

The sculptor, Grant Stevenson RA ARSA, specialised in large pieces and was a champion of Scottish sculpture, declining to take the more profitable highway south. He was an author too, and towards the end of this life – he died in 1919 – wrote a book of short stories, *Wee Johnnie Paterson and other Humorous Sketches* which was published by Foulis of Edinburgh.

**Robert Burns, Union Terrace, 1892**
Half way along the Terrace at the central entrance to the Gardens is a fine bronze statue of Robert Burns by Henry Bain Smith (1859–1896), an Aberdeen sculptor, who had served his apprenticeship as a stonecutter in Macdonald, Field & Co.'s granite yard in Constitution Street. Burns is shown addressing the mountain daisy held in his left hand, and at one time it became a fad, especially with students and GIs, to make off with the 'wee, modest crimson tippet flow'r.' Burns keeps warm on his pedestal of white Kemnay granite 'finely axed and of spotless purity' wearing a frock coat heavily pleated at the rear, with breeches and stockings, and a plaid slung over his jacket. His Tam o' Shanter, originally placed in his right hand, is back there, having at one point fallen down to his very large ploughman's feet. Thus the sculptor pays tribute to two of the Bard's most famous poems.

This was the largest piece of work attempted by Bain Smith, who specialised in small terracotta pieces, and heads and busts of well known figures such as Thomas Carlyle, historian and essayist, and locally, William Hall, the Footdee shipbuilder, Dr William Kidd, the celebrated Gilcomston preacher, James Saint the silk mercer and John Gray, founder of Gray's School of Art.

Burns' statue was accepted on behalf of the people of Aberdeen in September 1892 by the popular Lord Provost, David Stewart (not yet knighted) of Banchory Devenick, whose Aberdeen Comb Works in Causewayend were the largest in the world at that time. On the parapet beside the statue is Provost Stewart's recently matriculated coat of arms: two leopards' faces (for the city of Aberdeen) and a fess chequy and a lymphad (galley) for Stewart, beautifully cut in granite, in relief. Across the road, William Kelly's Aberdeen Savings Bank of 1895 on the corner

*The Burns statue and the Denburn Viaduct beyond, both when very new. Work is still going at the north end of the Gardens, below.*

*Lord Provost David Stewart's new coat-of-arms. It shares the site with Burns.*

with Diamond Place has a leopard head as the keystone of the handsome door. Kelly was perhaps inspired by Provost Stewart's arms opposite. The bank also has a down pipe embellished with little leopard faces, similar to, but more whiskery than those on Provost Stewart's coat of arms. Kelly also used his leopard keystone in his George Street Branch of the Aberdeen Savings Bank. This leopard 'movement' (the leopard in heraldry being similar to a lion) culminated in the *sejant gardant* cast-iron leopards which were designed by William Banbury for the extended Union Bridge of 1905 to 1908. They are known as Kelly's Cats, not because Dr Kelly designed them – though he is said to have designed the parapets – but apparently because he was outraged when he saw that students had tied ribbons around the leopards' necks one Charities' Week. He interpreted this as a discourtesy and ordered the ribbons to be removed forthwith. Hence the nickname. Or so the story goes. In another interesting link, one of Kelly's interior murals in his Union Terrace Savings Bank pays tribute to the famous Doric novel *Johnny Gibb of Gushetneuk*, which was written by William Alexander, editor of the *Aberdeen Free Press* – the very man who had organised the subscription to erect the Burns statue. The unveiling was performed by the famous and formidable David Masson, Professor of English at Edinburgh University, 'born little more than a stone cast from the spot where the statue stands.'

The sculptor Henry Bain Smith moved to England where his surname was elided to Bainsmith. He married a fellow artist, Georgina, and they had a son, Bruce. Bain Smith died unexpectedly in St John's Wood, London when he was only thirty-six. The brilliant Burns statue was to be his first and last large work and we are lucky to have it.

Robert Burns was a more suitable size and weight for Union Terrace than Wallace, and his arrival in 1892 completed the original row of statues between the Union Street/Terrace corner, and the Rosemount Viaduct triangle.

**King Edward VII Memorial, Union Street/Union Terrace Corner, 1914**
In 1914 Prince Albert and his chair were moved to the triangular extension of Union Terrace Gardens at Rosemount Viaduct, where he and William Wallace are within hailing distance of each other. Albert's original stance (or

rather sitz) at the Union Street/Terrace junction was thereafter dominated by Aberdeen's most elaborate group of statuary, the memorial to Victoria and Albert's son, Edward VII.

The monarch is dressed in the robes of the Order of the Garter and flanked by a sprinkling of emblematic figures, none of whom, with the exception of Britannia are dressed in anything at all. How did this curious tableau come about? The man behind it was Colonel Thomas Innes, 5th of Learney, who had been senior Royal Archer during the King's final visit to Scotland. He set in motion plans for a memorial to Edward to be erected in Aberdeen after the King's death. Memorial is the operative word, not statue, for Innes was adamant that this was to be the Scottish National Memorial to the King, celebrating Edward as monarch, emperor and peacemaker.

A fierce controversy arose over Innes' choice of the Union Street/Terrace site, already occupied by Albert. The Town initially offered the Colonel a site at Blackfriars Street at its junction with Schoolhill, where condemned housing was due for demolition (later the site of the War Memorial) but Innes, determined to have the best place in town, was not one to be gainsaid. The project went ahead. Prince Albert and chair were relocated and some structural alterations were carried out at his former site including the positioning of a pillar in the Gents' toilets in Union Terrace Gardens below, to support the weight of the statuary.

Colonel Innes, having initiated the creation of a Scottish memorial to the late king and possibly aware of the surge of interest in Scottish sculpture, nevertheless had chosen a Londoner, Alfred Drury RA, to design the proposed group of granite and bronze figures. Drury was described in the press as 'standing first among the English sculptors (in clay) of the day' and 'an artist of singularly refined and fastidious taste' noted for the 'beautiful lines of his female figures.' These included his bronze nude light standards in City Square, Leeds, and his much talked of nude lady playing the violincello. He had worked on important memorials in London and his specialities included historical and allegorical figures. The Edward VII commission was just his cup of tea. The memorial would allow him to indulge his penchant for tasteful nudes, personifications, and pomp and circumstance.

Drury sent up his plaster model for the statue of Edward VII from London to Arthur Taylor's granite yard in Jute Street, Aberdeen, where it was brilliantly carved from a block of Kemnay granite by one of Taylor's top craftsmen, James Philip. Britannia and the emblematic figures in the group, all bronze, were likely cast in Drury's own foundry. The memorial was inaugurated in 1914, four years after Edward's death and two years after Colonel Innes' own demise at ninety-eight.

On a plinth of polished red Peterhead granite, Edward, in contrasting white Kemnay granite, holds the sceptre and orb. The ornate knickerbockers of his garter ensemble are handsomely carved by Philip who has also endowed his granite cloak with a feeling of fluidity. If one looks closely, just

*Edward takes shape in Arthur Taylor's granite yard in Jute Street, Aberdeen. James Philip, right, is working on the King with a hand puncheon.*

# THE VERY PLACE FOR STATUES

*King Edward and companions. Union Terrace Gardens lies below.*

below His Majesty is the Scottish touch, a tiny figure of St Andrew, the patron saint, in a shield-shaped miniature, virtually entrapped by his cross. The bronze group on the west side is dominated by Britannia, representing Peace, and struggling to break a sword. Its point is held down to the ground but the blade bulges under pressure, perilously close to the bare toes of her sandaled foot. The Angel of Peace looks on with interest, his wings neatly folded. Above them in bronze hand-tooled lettering are the words 'Australia and New Zealand'. Moving round, the rear of the memorial overlooking Union Terrace Gardens is blank, apart from another bronze nameplate, reading 'South and West Africa'. Finally, the group on the east side shows a curly-headed naked African boy trying to present Britannia with a posy of roses, while one of Alfred Drury's delightful young ladies,

*Britannia attempts to break a sword while the Angel of Peace offers encouragement.*

naked apart from her pigtails, reaches up to Britannia. The bronze lettering reads 'Newfoundland and Canada'. One's initial assumption is that these statues are personifications of the realms of the British Empire indicated in the bronze lettering. But they don't appear to correspond. The African boy and pigtailed girl, for example, do not seem appropriate representatives for Newfoundland and Canada.

These days, Edward VII's stock has risen, particularly regarding his skills in diplomacy and in stimulating international friendship. The memorial might have been of greater historical interest if Drury could have forsaken his stock-in-trade personifications and given us some genuine empire and colonial figures of the time. He could create a life-like, fully clad artilleryman, so a maharaja, tribal chief, trapper and gold miner for example, should not have been beyond his range, while Edward could have been portrayed in the kilt and Glengarry that he wore while in residence at Balmoral.

Regardless of its shortcomings however, one can appreciate the heroic sweep and flow of the Edward Memorial. White granite, grey granite, the deep pink of the plinth, gold accoutrements and dark bronzes all blend soberly rather than gaudily, curving neatly into the balustraded semi-circle above the Gents'. The best view is from the middle of Union Street, undertaken from the safety of a bus heading east. Perhaps with a bit of readjustment, this piece of statuary could provide a sumptuous entrance to Union Terrace Gardens.

### Albert, the Prince Consort, resettled at the triangle, 1914

The sedentary life of Prince Albert's statue at the Union Terrace corner had not been without incident. There had been some commotion in 1892 when ornate Gents' toilets were installed in the Gardens, immediately below. A greater upset came in 1914 when he was ousted altogether in favour of the elaborate memorial to his son. He now sits a trifle uncomfortably near the edge of the grass on the Rosemount Viaduct triangle facing Union Terrace but his repositioning there offers an interesting bonus for anyone walking past. A closer inspection of the statue is allowed compared with those on high plinths. It is a very fine piece of work with the Prince in Field Marshall's robes, with high boots and feathered hat in hand, wearing the insignia of

*Prince Albert re-sited at the Union Terrace Gardens 'triangle'.*

the Thistle and holding the scroll recalling his speech as President to the British Association in Aberdeen's newly built Music Hall in 1859. Designed by James Matthews, the pristine Music Hall fitted seamlessly at the rear of the Assembly Rooms and Prince Albert had presided over the opening ceremony.

Albert's statue, in its original position, was the first contribution to that excellent and irreplaceable group of statuary that runs from the Union Street/Terrace corner, along the Terrace to Robert Burns, to William Wallace at the Rosemount triangle, not forgetting General Gordon of Khartoum, outside Robert Gordon's College. These statues have created a unique setting for Union Terrace Gardens and the area around and are important in their own right, historically and as works of art.

**Postscript: Gordon of Khartoum, 1888**

A fine statue of Gordon of Khartoum (1833–1885) stands in the Schoolhill pocket park outside Robert Gordon's College though it has nothing to do with the school apart from the name being the same. The link is with the Gordon clan which funded the statue and gifted it to the city. When news of Gordon's heroic death at Khartoum in Sudan at the hands of the dervishes reached this country, it triggered a sympathetic 'wave of public grief'. Members of Clan Gordon the leading clan in the North-east, headed by the Marquis of Huntly enthusiastically decided to erect a statue to the legendary general. Appreciation of his heroism did not extend to the sporrans of all Clan Gordon members, however. A year had elapsed by March 1886 and donations totalled only £492 11s 2d. Apparently a good bronze statue 'could not be had for less than £700.' The cost of the plinth and a suitable site would bring the total up to £1,000. A further whip round was organised, and the Edinburgh sculptor, T Stuart Burnett ARSA (1853–1888) agreed 'to accept a comparatively small figure for his work.' James Matthews got on with choosing and designing the plinth. Of deep pink Correnie granite, it matches the beautiful façade behind it.

*General Gordon of Khartoum.*

# UNION TERRACE GARDENS

The late General's brother and sister, who must have been overwhelmed at the number of Gordon memorials springing up all over the country, nevertheless had the highest of praise for the Aberdeen work and were particularly impressed by the likeness. Burnett obviously did not stint his efforts in spite of the low fee. Sadly he died before the statue was unveiled by the Marquis of Huntly in June 1888 when Clan Gordon handed it over to the Town Council as representatives of the people of Aberdeen. The clan had opted to erect the statue outside Gordon's College and the Town Council were happy to agree.

## Lord Byron

It might be appropriate to see the statue of another famous Gordon, George Gordon, Lord Byron sharing the pocket park, positioned to General Gordon's left in front of the former Gray's School of Art. Gray's was built on the site of the old Grammar School that Byron attended. He died in 1824, and so never was a pupil at the 'new' Aberdeen Grammar of 1863 in whose grounds his statue, mainly by Pittendreich Macgillivray, currently stands. That statue is a fine one, but cannot be fully appreciated from the road.

*Lord Byron's statue could take up residence alongside General Gordon's.*

CHAPTER EIGHT

# JOHN GRAY 1811–1891
## THE IDEAL BENEFACTOR

*John Gray.*

It is very fitting to note here the name of John Gray perhaps the most open-handed of the Aberdeen's benefactors and the founder of the School of Art which bears his name. Along with the Scott Sutherland School of Architecture, Gray's is perhaps the most renowned of the Schools of the Robert Gordon University. Since 1966 it has been located at Garthdee where Henry Bain Smith's neat and elegant bust of Gray will greet you at the School's entrance. Born in Cuminestown in 1811, the son of a carpenter and millwright, Gray learnt the elements of his father's trade as a young lad, came to Aberdeen to seek his fortune and found part-time employment at the firm of William Mackinnon & Co., ironfounders of Spring Garden (there is a well known photograph of great teams of horses, carts and carters lined up outside the long frontage of the firm). The Mackinnons, much impressed by Gray's commitment and skill, subsequently offered him full-time employment in the pattern shop. In time he became a partner, then head of the firm. He was over fifty by that time, homely, unpretentious and speaking his native Doric as most local people still did. Though he was an excellent businessman and in the course of his career did much to expand the range of Mackinnon's expertise, he did not care greatly for public life. A town councillor from 1869 to 1872 and again from 1880 to 1888, he was a reluctant Master of the Guild Brethern's Hospital and Convener of the Water Committee, and would not on any account be persuaded to become a baillie. But an earlier appointment, made in 1859, as a director of the Aberdeen Mechanics Institute, was one after his own heart. As a youth he had been frustrated by his lack of technical training and doubtless wished he could have attended such a place. The Institute had a library which Gray regarded of prime importance, and was developing an educational programme and organising local art classes but the building was cramped and dated. Gray felt it would be desirable to have a specific school dedicated to the teaching of Science and Art.

He had his site earmarked, beside the city's proposed Art Gallery, and seized the initiative. The ground was on the east side of the Robert Gordon's College entrance in Schoolhill (it ceased to be Robert Gordon's Hospital in 1881) where Byron's old Grammar School was still standing. He wrote to the Lord Provost Peter Esslemont, who was also President of the Governors of the fledgling Robert Gordon's College, proposing 'to erect at my own cost [this came to around £5,000] on said site a School for Science and Art for behoof of the community of Aberdeen, in harmony with the design of the Art Gallery, according to the accompanying plan prepared by Messrs Matthews & Mackenzie, Architects.' Gray continued, 'On this plan it will be observed that an arched Gateway is shown connecting the Art Gallery and the proposed School. This is part of the scheme I should like to see carried out, but it appears to me that it falls more properly to be taken up by the Governors of Robert Gordon's College and either by themselves or in conjunction with the Art Gallery Committee.'

*The newly completed Schoolhill frontage with Gray's School of Art, right.*

*The pocket park was later created for General Gordon's statue.*

*The Central School was built opposite the Gordon's frontage on the site Gray failed to acquire for his Public Library. The East Free of the Triple Kirks is on the right, with Union Terrace Gardens just out of range. General Gordon stands alone in the pocket park, awaiting Lord Byron perhaps?*

He was far from pushy, adopting a gently-gently approach, but he knew what exactly he wanted, and his proposals were adopted. Byron's old Grammar came down and Gray bears much responsibility for the creation of the famous arched gateway, the focal point of the façade, as well, of course, as his School of Art.

A great believer in the concept of free public libraries, Gray was instrumental in persuading the Dunfermline-born tycoon Andrew Carnegie of Pittsburgh, an outstanding benefactor of public libraries, to donate liberally to the new Aberdeen Public Library as he had done himself. He had hoped to have the library built on the site opposite Gordon's College where the Central School (now the 'Academy' mall) eventually went up, which would have allowed him to give even greater unity to the area. He was

*Gray eventually acquired a magnificent site on the new Viaduct for his Library, left, and South Free Kirk. The Royal Infirmary, Woolmanhill, is to the rear with the Wallace Statue extreme right.*

unsuccessful however and settled for the new embankment at Rosemount Viaduct, opposite the north end of Union Terrace, and this proved a perfect site. The library, which opened in 1891, had a total cost of over £10,000. Gray was able to persuade Carnegie to perform at the opening ceremony, though that was not held until 1892, by which time, sadly, Gray was dead.

Gray was also a member of the kirk session of the South Free, and began the exodus of the Triple Kirks from the Denburn Valley. He gave £3,000 towards the erection of a new, roomier church next to the Public Library at Rosemount Viaduct, a stone's throw from the Triple Kirks. It had become quite the fashion for new churches to be built in the west end. The West Free on the corner of Union Street and Bon Accord Street was a good example, as was the magnificent Carden Place United Free, 'the Cathedral Church of the United Presbyterians,' whose congregation moved west from a simple warehouse-style building in George Street. Gray made it a condition of his contribution that the new South Free should be in the same locality as the old. Sadly he died in that year of 1891 and did not live to see the completion of his kirk.

Chapter Nine

# DISRUPTION IN THE DENBURN VALLEY

**The Mutton Brae and the Schoolhill Factory, the Corinthian University, the Triple Kirks and the Denburn Valley Junction Railway**

Across the Denburn Valley, on the east side, life had not stood still. By the late eighteenth century, the Mutton Brae was a sizeable settlement of poor but picturesque pantiled houses, or stern and formidable slums, depending on which illustration you looked at. They clung to the cliffside, which was not yet eroded when they were built and whatever you thought of it, Mutton Brae had an excellent position, dominating the Denburn Valley.

According to GM Fraser the first Mutton Brae house was probably built 'upon the piece of ground lying on the south side of Schoolhill' granted in 1749 to George Smith, blacksmith. Other houses went up, scattered around Schoolhill, Woolmanhill and the future Blackfriars Street. These are visible on Wood's Map of 1821 (page 41) opposite Denburn Terrace. 'Belmount Street' is fairly well developed with its long gardens going down to the Denburnside. The bathhouse is still there. But stretching between 'Denburn' and the end of 'Belmount Street' it looks as if a village (unnamed) had appeared. Mutton Brae, for it was surely the village in question, seems to have solidified into a settlement and the long black shape beside the scattered houses and above the Brae on the map could well be the grim Schoolhill Handloom Factory. Mutton Brae, whatever its origin, was conveniently sited to become a handloom weavers' village and most of Mutton Brae's inhabitants either worked in the neighbouring Schoolhill Handloom Factory, or in their own homes. The poet William Cadenhead presents an idealised picture of the Factory. In his 'Lays of Bon Accord' he writes:

*a hive*
*O happy weavers aince did thrive;*
*Wha's fair day's wark did mair than earn*
*A scanty meal for wife and bairn,*
*And left a clushach i' the moggan*
*In times o stress to keep them joggin*
*Or help a needy neebour through.*

clushach: money saved

moggan: old stocking leg used to hoard money

Cadenhead used to be an overseer at Broadford and perhaps liked to think that all millworkers were happy and content. Nevertheless, during its forty-five years of existence the Schoolhill Factory enjoyed a bad reputation. Possibly its best known employee was the handloom-weaver poet, Willie Thom, author of *The Blind Boy's Pranks* (1841) and *Rhymes and Recollections of a Handloom Weaver* which went to three editions during the 1840s. His memories were bitter. He writes of those 'who knew the misery, the destroying influences that during nearly a century [ie the forty-five years of the Factory's existence] were upheld and nourished within the dismal walls of the Schoolhill Factory.' After Thom left the handloom factory he was fêted throughout Scotland when his works were published, but his new-found wealth was quickly dissipated. Deserted by his hangers-on, he died in poverty in Dundee in 1848. Another renowned but more successful graduate of the handloom factory was Professor Alexander Bain, the founder of modern psychology and first holder of the Chair of Logic and Rhetoric at Aberdeen University. He lived in Gilcomston as a boy and was said to have started his earlier career as a handloom weaver at Schoolhill. He was only twelve when the factory closed so he could not have worked there for more than two years.

With the introduction of sophisticated power looms into the Aberdeen and Woodside mills in the 1820s the writing was on the wall for the Schoolhill Factory. It was stopped in 1830. No master would pay these handloom weavers more than their own operatives at Woodside who did the same work more quickly for less money. It was an end of a way of life for most of the Schoolhill weavers, though the best of them were likely taken on at the Woodside Works to be trained up to use the power looms. Ordinary working folk moved into Mutton Brae, in addition to the 'characters' who were there even in the days of the weavers.

The journalist Robert Anderson had mixed feelings about the place. In *Aberdeen in Bygone Days* he commented, 'Truth to tell it was a poor, miserable and rather squalid thoroughfare, albeit there was a certain old-fashioned quaintness.' William Smith of *The Bon Accord* wrote:

> It was for long, one of the many clusters of artisans' dwellings that were in the suburbs of the city; and in every other house might be heard the clatter of the weaver's loom. The houses sat about in a higgledy-piggledy manner, just for all the earth as if they had been built in the Schoolhill and then slid down the brae to settle as chance happened. They were all shapes and sizes, gable-ends and outside stairs being their most conspicuous architectural feature, while a bit of colour was added by many of the structures being red-tile, so the cluster of modest dwellings on the break-neck brae had a most picturesque appearance.

Mutton Brae may not have been as haphazard as Smith would have us believe. There was a Back Brae, a Middle Brae and a Front Brae, where, apparently, the 'better class of tradesman' resided. Mrs Mary Hall kept a byre and some beasts on the Front Brae, as well as a hut where she had her store of neeps for the cows. She kept Mutton Brae in milk and butter for years. The Brae was a friendly place for most. There would be soirées in the brick-floored kitchens where fiddlers would play and the young people would dance.

'It was almost a village separate from Aberdeen,' recalled another commentator. 'Its older inhabitants clustered of a summer evening for a smoke and chat round the Corbie Well in a quietude that was undisturbed by shunting locomotives and had not yet been turned into Union Terrace Gardens with their pleasance of tree-shaded walks and parterres.' John

*Shabby houses near the north-east corner of Union Terrace Gardens. Mutton Brae, left, and a glimpse of Union Bridge, centre, and the south end of the Gardens, right.*

*The grim photograph (left) makes a contrast with John Bulloch's charming watercolour of the same view of Mutton Brae and the Triple Kirks. Note the decoration on the spire. The weavers had left by the time the Triple Kirks were built.*

Bulloch, a distinguished local literary figure of the time, editor of the *Aberdeen Magazine* and *Scottish Notes and Queries* and author of a biography of the portrait painter George Jamesone, was a Sunday School teacher in Mutton Brae as a young man. The room he used was also the meeting place of the St James Lodge of Masons. He made a delightful 'primitive' sketch of the village.

By the mid-1820s, the architect Archibald Simpson was installed in new offices at No. 132 Union Street, on the Belmont Street corner, which he had designed himself. He was working on plans for a new Marischal College. No major repairs had been carried out at the old Broad Street building for the best part of a century, and the Duke of Cumberland could not be lodged there in 1746, because the rooms were so damp. In 1824 the Royal Commission on Scottish Universities invited Simpson and John Smith, the city architect, to submit schemes for a new building. Smith, who had recently designed a new frontage for King's College in Old Aberdeen,

*Looking across to the Corinthian University from Union Bridge, with its original balustrades. This 'artist's impression' was by Simpson's friend, James Giles.*

politely bowed out and left the field open for Simpson who prepared several schemes for a site on Union Street between Bridge Street and Crown Street, others for the current Broad Street site, and for the Schoolhill Factory site. Even though the factory was still in operation Simpson would have been aware of advances in the weaving trade and known that the days of the handloom were numbered. He was also aware of the factory's spectacular site, dominating the Denburn Valley.

The Committee of Professors overseeing the development had specified 'Grecian architecture' and Simpson seems to have envisaged a graceful swan emerging from the rubble of the ugly duckling of the old weaving shed, that 'prime nursery of vice and sorrow' as Willie Thom had called it. The Corinthian Scheme, as the new design was known, was not at all Simpsonesque. Our illustration shows a hexastyle (six pillared) portico set forward and further extended by columns on either side forming an elegant colonnade. The columns were in the Corinthian idiom, their capitals enriched by carved acanthus leaves. Chunky endpieces mimicked the Cromwell Tower at King's College on a reduced scale. Vying with the colonnade for attention and probably winning, was a massive central dome supported by a robust 'drum' below and a 'lantern' above, to light the upper storey. The natural levels of the Denburn Valley are used, and on the illustration one can make out an arcaded basement on the left, probably completely exposed for the length of the building though one can't see for the trees. Its roof forms the terrace of the main colonnaded area, where tiny figures are walking.

This favoured scheme suffered a variety of delays and vicissitudes including, for a time, the unsuccessful re-emergence of demands for the union of King's and Marischal Colleges, interruptions by visits from the King's architect and Royal Commissions, Treasury delays, plans going astray, problems with Exchequer grants and escalating costs and in 1826, a fire at Simpson's office. Neighbours and passers-by tried to extinguish it by forming a chain down Patagonian Court, and passing up buckets of water from the Denburn, but to no avail. There was a disastrous loss of Simpson's plans, papers and books. He bounced back in due course, restored his office, added a twin, and the double block became Nos 122–132 Union Street.

The Corinthian Scheme, however, was deemed too expensive and rejected but all was not lost. Simpson's less costly plans for a new Marischal College Quad on the old Broad Street site were chosen, and built between 1836 and 1841. It is still there, quietly elegant, behind the magnificent façade. The architect also modified his plans for the Corinthian University, and it emerged in 1827 as Stracathro House in Angus for the wealthy Mr Alexander Cruickshank, minus the dome and with a slightly more modest portico.

The Triple Kirks was one of the most amazing products of the Disruption of 1843 which split the Church of Scotland and led to the establishment of the Free Kirk. The dispute had been simmering for some time. The main issue was that of patronage, the right of the patron, be he the local laird or the town council, to appoint a minister to a parish church without taking into consideration the preferences of the congregation. In Aberdeen the patron of the city's six *quoad civilia* kirks (those with full parish status) was the Town Council itself which, since the Reformation, had never gone against the wishes of the congregation when appointing a new minister. The other nine churches in the city were *quoad sacra* (kirks but with religious status only) and already had the 'freedom' of choosing their own minister. Even so, all fifteen Aberdeen ministers and many of their congregations 'came out' – as the physical act of leaving the kirk was described – in May 1843. It was simply a gesture of solidarity against state interference, for in Aberdeen the battle was already won, while across Scotland, 450 ministers came out. No fewer than ten new Free Kirks were built in the city in this period, for many of those who came out were members of the city's business community, with the energy, zeal and money to organise the building and the funding. (To end this part of the story, the system of patronage was abolished in 1874, and the Church of Scotland and the Free Kirk were re-united in 1929, bequeathing Aberdeen two churches in every parish).

Returning to 1843, the Disruption, one of the most stirring events in Aberdeen's history, had been foreseen for some time, and activists had the matter well in hand. A Joint Local Provisional Committee had been set up to look for suitable sites for the new Free Kirks and the lawyer Francis Edmond, though still an elder of the West Kirk of St Nicholas, had, in April 1843, bought Gordon Barron's old Schoolhill weaving factory which had lain derelict since its closure thirteen years earlier. That was a month before the great exodus that marked the start of the Disruption, so Edmond was ahead of the game. The factory was quickly demolished. The women of Mutton Brae were allowed to take away the timber when the buildings were being pulled down and some were injured in the scramble.

The services of Archibald Simpson had been booked in advance. Few knew the old factory site better than he. He had the plans drawn up, worked out estimates, organised the widening of Schoolhill, and designed an amazing complex of three Free Kirks, sharing a single granite-lined brick spire. The new Free Kirks would serve the former congregations of the churches of the nearby East and West parishes of St Nicholas, and of the South parish church (now 'Slains Castle') which was a stone's throw away on Belmont

*Archibald Simpson by James Giles. The Triple Kirks, of which he was particularly proud, looms in the background, with another of his specials, the Infirmary at Woolmanhill, glimpsed beyond. The view would have been from a rear window in his Union Street office.*

Street, shoehorned between Little Belmont Street and Gaelic Lane. There were 3,446 worshipers all told, and most were expected to come out. There would be seats for all in the new Free Kirks. The East Free was finished by December 1843, just seven months after the exodus, the West Free the following January, and the South Free a little later. The Triple Kirks would subsequently be described as 'the only church in Scotland purpose-built to house three separate congregations.' Three separate churches sharing a spire would be more accurate.

*The Triple Kirks. An ethereal interpretation by James Giles. The trees in the Belmont Street back gardens are flourishing. Courtesy of Aberdeen City Libraries.*

The Triple Kirks, as breathtaking a sight as the Corinthian University would have been, dominated the north-east end of Denburn Valley. In spite of the fact that it was anti-Disruption, the *Aberdeen Herald* newspaper expounded: 'A group of three churches when viewed from Union Bridge has the aspect of a cathedral . . . In the angle formed by the nave and south transept rises a lofty square tower, from which springs a spire of airy proportions . . . the elevation from the Denburn being 204 feet.' Simpson had based his design of the spire on that of medieval St Elizabeth Kirche of Marburg in Prussia – now Hesse in Germany. The librarian-historian GM Fraser writes, 'I confess I received rather a shock when it was brought to my notice with photographic illustrations by one of our Aberdeen architects that Simpson's is not an original design but a copy of one of the twin steeples at the western end of the church of St Elizabeth, Marburg. It must have appealed to Archibald Simpson in an especial degree for he copied the most western steeple most faithfully for Belmont Street.' There is no record of Simpson visiting Marburg. He would have consulted an architect's pattern book with illustrations of brick spires.

# DISRUPTION IN THE DENBURN VALLEY

*The twin spires of the St Elizabeth Kirche of Marburg which Simpson copied.*

Even Willie Thom had something good to say about this ecclesiastical phenomenon. In his *Recollections* he wrote, 'Among the many stately buildings that now claim a stranger's notice as he approaches Aberdeen from the south, most of all will he admire the cluster of churches lately erected at the north end of Belmont Street. The chance is even grateful to the eye when one remembers the odious-looking rickles that for seventy (*sic*) long years disfigured that spot.'

Speed and economy had been watchwords in designing the Triple Kirks. The total cost was only around £6,000. They were built of granite rubble, some of it from the down-takings of the Schoolhill Factory while the bricks of the spire were from the Seaton Brick Works, some say the Clayhills, near Ferryhill. Given the mongrel nature of the building materials it was a very considerable achievement that the masonry appeared as uniform as it did. The Triple Kirks are Category A listed, on the strength of their design alone. Had they been built of dressed granite their fate may not have been such a problem for the city. Nevertheless at the time of the Disruption and for long afterwards their beauty and elegance made a great impression on Aberdonians and visitors alike.

# UNION TERRACE GARDENS

\*\*\*

**Mary Slessor**

The world-famous Aberdeen-born missionary Mary Slessor (1848–1915) one of Scotland's greatest daughters and a national heroine in Nigeria, would have known the Corbie Heugh well. According to some reports she was born in Short Loanings in nearby Gilcomston, but the family soon moved to Mutton Brae, the weavers' little settlement beside the Triple Kirks, at that time in their infancy. Her father was a drunken souter who had difficulty in holding down a job; her mother, a skilled handloom weaver who bore the burdens of breadwinner and bringing up a large family. Mary attended the old Belmont Street Free Church, a Secessionist kirk, later United Free (UF) which stood just opposite the Triple Kirks and Mutton Brae.

The family moved to Dundee in search of work in 1859 when Mary was eleven. Here she worked in the weaving mills but devoted what spare time she had to reading about the Christian faith and about missionary work in which the UF Kirk was much involved. After hearing the news of David Livingstone's death, she decided to train as a missionary, and was sent to Calabar in Nigeria in 1876, where the UF Kirk had a presence. Her achievements both practical and reforming there were amazing. She worked tirelessly to protect children and took in those that were unwanted, especially twins, who were liable to be done away with. She promoted the position of women in African tribal society, became a teacher, mediator and eventually a colonial official presiding over the native court in Okoyong where she had been appointed vice-consul. In 1913 she was awarded the Order of St John of Jerusalem. Over the years she had suffered increasingly severe bouts of malaria and eventually became too weak to return to Scotland as she had once hoped to do. There was great mourning at her passing in 1915 and she was given the colonial equivalent of a state funeral in Duke Town, Calabar, attended by high-ranking colonial officials. A Union Flag covered her coffin.

The lowest level of the Gardens contains a small circular, finely crafted memorial to Mary Slessor in Kemnay granite, encircled by granite sets.

# DISRUPTION IN THE DENBURN VALLEY

*The small, circular memorial to Mary Slessor is visible in the middle distance.*

*A Clydesdale Bank £10 note commemorating Mary Slessor.*

*The service of celebration at the Mary Slessor Memorial on 13 January, 2015.*

Designed by Mary Bourne, it can be clearly viewed from Union Terrace as well as from ground level. In Belmont Street a fragment of the kirk that succeeded Mary Slessor's original kirk, Belmont Street UF, has been incorporated into the wall of 'The Academy' shopping centre, and here Mary is also commemorated by a plaque. Her portrait has graced the £10 note of the Clydesdale Bank.

The year 2015 marked the centenary of her death. A service celebrating her life and work took place at the Mary Slessor Memorial in Union Terrace Gardens on the date of her death, 13 January, led by Dr Mark Igiehon. He said, 'She made an amazing difference to the lives of Nigerian women and she is still greatly revered there today.'

\*\*\*

# DISRUPTION IN THE DENBURN VALLEY

**The Denburn Valley Junction Railway**

Twenty or so years after the Disruption of the Church of Scotland there arrived a disruption of another sort. The railway came to the Denburn Valley and the quietude was about to be disturbed by these shunting locomotives. The Aberdeen Railway Company, connecting Aberdeen with the south, opened a temporary terminus at Ferryhill in 1850, extending to a new terminus, shared with the Deeside Railway, on Guild Street in August 1854. By 1855 the GNSR serving points north had extended from its first terminus at Kittybrewster, at this point following the bed of the Aberdeenshire Canal, to Waterloo Quay. The two separate stations in Aberdeen, Guild Street and Waterloo Quay, were inconvenient not only for passengers but also for transfer of the goods wagons which had to be pulled by horses along the quays on tracks belonging to Aberdeen Harbour Commissioners. Mail was conveyed by fast gig between the two stations, but if trains from the south were late, Great North staff were reputedly instructed to ensure punctual departure of their own services, even if potential passengers were seen hurrying to the station. Doors were slammed in their faces. There were many complaints.

The obvious answer was a line from Kittybrewster to Guild Street, entering the Denburn Valley south of Woolmanhill and exiting under Union Bridge. This would be costly to build, and negotiations between the GNSR and the Scottish North Eastern Railway (SNER), successors to the Aberdeen Railway, broke down, leading to rival schemes being promoted in 1862. The SNER proposed a line from Limpet Mill near Stonehaven to Kintore, also connecting with the Deeside Railway near Culter. The GNSR's scheme was the hugely controversial 'Circumbendibus Railway' which would have entailed construction of a cutting, referred to in the *Aberdeen Journal* as an 'unsightly ditch', from Kittybrewster to Clayhills via Rosemount, the city's west end and Ferryhill. The furore created in the city was almost of the scale of the Union Terrace Gardens controversy 150 years later. Common sense eventually prevailed and Parliamentary powers were obtained by way of the Denburn Valley Railway Act passed on 23 June 1864. The GNSR subscribed £125,000 and the SNER, which was subsequently absorbed by the Caledonian Railway, put in £70,000. The double-track line was built between 1865 and 1867. In the valley itself the Denburn was culverted first

*The Denburn is culverted. Courtesy of Aberdeen City Libraries.*

to run along the west side of the tracks for about two-thirds of the length of the valley. It then crossed to run down the east side, under Union Bridge, along the west side of the Green and eventually to the Upper Dock.

Much of the design work for the Denburn line was undertaken by John Willet CE, an Ayrshire man 'of a kindly and cheerful bearing towards all with whom he came in contact.' His career as a Civil Engineer had been devoted to the construction of new railways for the burgeoning private companies of the day and he came to Aberdeen in 1847 two years after being appointed engineer of the Caledonian Railway. By a curious coincidence in 1860, Willet was due to take up residence in a new house, No. 30 Albyn Place, through which the Circumbendibus was due to run. However, completion of the house was delayed for nearly two years when the project was eventually abandoned. Willet was then able to move into the Albyn Place house as planned.

He worked on the Denburn Valley Line between 1865 and 1867,

# DISRUPTION IN THE DENBURN VALLEY

*The tracks for the Denburn Valley Junction Railway are laid. Courtesy of Aberdeen City Libraries.*

building tunnels at Woolmanhill and at Maberley Street–Hutcheon Street. Around 120 houses had to be demolished, mainly in Mutton Brae, but in Woolmanhill and the Lower Denburn as well. At the same time Willet designed Bridge Street as an elevated thoroughfare to connect Union Street with the Joint Station of 1867. The new road was brought down from Union Street to Guild Street by a viaduct of arches, gradually decreasing in height for most of the way. One of these arches carried the new road over Windmill Brae. By the 1880s Willet had moved to a house in Union Terrace, where he was able to keep his eye on the Denburn Valley Railway from his window.

Journey's end for the Denburn Valley Line was the first Joint Station. 'Joint' for it was shared by the lines from the north and the south. It had one long through-platform, three further through-tracks and two short bay platforms at each end for local trains and a large curved roof supposedly modelled on the roof of London Victoria Station. Despite some improvements over the years it was always inadequate for the increased traffic generated. A major rebuild eventually took place between 1912 and 1915 when the new structure was largely completed. To complete the story, most of the 1915 station still survives despite major remodelling in the 1980s and over the last few years as part of the Union Square development. The Joint Station, as it has been known to many generations of Aberdonians, still plays an important role in Aberdeen's transport infrastructure.

Returning to Mutton Brae, the colony had not experienced good times. The original steepness of the east side of the Valley had been eroded by the laying out of the 'Backs of Belmont', the buildings and gardens at the back of the west side of Belmont Street. The village had experienced disturbance during the building of the Triple Kirks and all that remained when the Denburn Valley Railway was completed in 1867 was a small group of houses and a pub, wedged into the south-west corner of the Denburn Valley. The little colony which had narrowly survived earlier clearances was completely wiped out by the building of the Rosemount Viaduct, as we have seen. By 1886, their livelihood and now their homes taken from them, all inhabitants had dispersed.

Denburn Road, which had developed from the original gravel walk on the east side of the Denburn, had to be diverted to accommodate the railway, and came very close to the gable of the West Free. There followed a great public outcry that the railway cutting was too close to the kirk, that the gable was in danger of collapse, and that there were 'rents in the building.' To test for vibration, tumblers of water were placed in doorways on the west side of the kirk, and railway engines were raced up and down.

The result of this experiment was never revealed, but the congregation of the West Free, fearful that their building was now undermined, migrated to the old Gilcomston Free Kirk premises in Huntly while steel tie rods were inserted at the base of the West Free to keep it from falling down. Meanwhile long drawn-out negotiations had been going on between the Kirks and the GNSR with the outcome that the railway company purchased the Triple

Kirks for £12,000 – double the original purchase price. The East and the South Free repurchased their kirks for £3,000 each, a profit of £1,000 per church. Most of the West Free congregation did not return to their old haunts, but now with money in hand, bought and demolished a house at the corner of Union and Bon Accord Streets, and built a new church there and gave it the old name, the West Free. The GNSR money was well spent for it was a handsome kirk. The Rose Window above the pulpit was famous in its day – the first stained glass in any of the Free Kirks in Aberdeen. It caused quite a stushie in some Free enclaves. It was considered to 'savour of popery.' The new West Free later became the West Church of St Andrew, then the Langstane Kirk, remembered for the annual sale of paintings in the forecourt, once the garden of the old house. It is now Soul Bar restaurant and casino. The later stained-glass windows were the work of John M Aitken over several years. They are brilliant – one of Aberdeen's hidden treasures.

The game of Disruption musical chairs continued when a minority group from the West Free bought back their old church at the Triple Kirks for £3,800 – not such a good deal as that achieved by the two stay-at-home kirks, but these chipped in a total of £2,000, which was of great assistance to the splinter group. The congregation wanted to rename their kirk the 'Old Free West', but the presbytery would not allow the use of 'West', so in 1867 it became the High Free Church.

In 1890 the smallest of the three kirks, the South Free, which had an expanding and a distinguished congregation, acquired a prime site, thanks to the largesse of the iron founder, John Gray, adjacent to the Public Library in the newly laid out Rosemount Viaduct. The East Free then acquired the former South Free premises and the architect William Kelly was commissioned to convert them into a suite of halls and classrooms. So now it was just the Double Kirks, the East Free and the High Free. In 1900 the Free and the United Presbyterian Churches joined forces throughout the country and in 1922 Belmont Street United Free, a fine little church which was built on a part of the Caberstone Croft in Belmont Street in 1779, united with the East United Free at the Triple Kirks site to become the East Free and Belmont. Meanwhile in 1935, the High Free had moved to Hilton and became High Hilton. With the development of the former Hilton Estate for housing, many families from the city's central area had moved there, and were in need of a kirk. The old building was subsequently occupied by an all-male religious group. And that left just the single kirk, the East Free and Belmont. In 1950, after the male religious group departed, the former West Free/High Free building was purchased by Albion and St Paul's Congregational Church which sixteen years later united with Belmont Congregational Church (formerly Chapel), with the latter's premises becoming the chosen place of worship as St Nicholas Congregational Church. And so the old West Free building was left unoccupied. And because of a decline in congregational strengths in central Aberdeen, it was sensible for East and Belmont to unite with their near neighbour in Rosemount Viaduct, the South United Free, the first of the Triple Kirks to flit. The new charge became St Marks, as it remains. And so there were no kirks left in the Triple Kirks.

Chapter Ten

# TURRETS, TOWERS, SPIRES, DOMES, DIESELS AND DUAL CARRIAGEWAY

I can remember when I first became conscious of the Triple Kirks though they were no longer referred to by their original names. In those distant days soon after the Second World War I was quite small and family members – I think we had been attending a wedding – were looking from a window in the lounge of the Caledonian Hotel across to Union Terrace Gardens. An argument was in full swing. Disagreement centred not round the 'eyesore' state of these kirks, for they were still going strong, but about the fact that the common spire was built of brick, and therefore, my aunt argued, was a blot on the landscape of the Granite City. It had no right to be there. My uncle

*The view from the Caledonian Thistle Hotel.*

maintained that the steeple, both powerful and handsome, gave presence to the cluster of kirks. It would be sadly missed if it ever disappeared. The episode stuck in my mind, and I kept an eye on the red brick spire whenever I was going along Union Terrace with my mother to the Savings Bank or the Public Library to make sure that it was still there.

Uncle John was by no means the only admirer of the Triple's spire. The poet John Betjeman was in Aberdeen a little later, and wrote of Archibald Simpson in *First and Last Loves* (1952):

> His greatest work is a brick tower and spire opposite the Art Gallery. The fact that it is in red brick makes it stand out, but not glaringly, among the grey granite of the rest of the city. How can I explain why this tall plain spire is so marvellous that only Salisbury is in my opinion its rival?

He also wrote of the spire glowing red in the setting sun: 'It is visible from a great many places in central Aberdeen and is a key component of the parade of turrets, towers and spires along Belmont Street and eastward,

*'The aspect of a German cathedral city.' The rear elevations of Belmont Street, looking across Union Terrace Gardens c.1870. Courtesy of Aberdeen City Libraries.*

presenting the aspect of a German Mitteleuropa cathedral city.' Right enough, Archibald Simpson's model for the spire was that of the St Elizabeth Kirche, which was in Prussia in his day.

My own next memory of the Kirks came years later, passing by with a friend when they were in the early days of their abandonment. The doors of Albion and St Paul's – the old West Free – were open and we wandered inside. It was a doleful scene. There were puddles of water everywhere and signs of dry rot. Unused communion cards were scattered all over the place. A number of illustrated wood-framed Cradle Rolls and advertisements for forthcoming meetings were lying around. It seemed a shame to leave them to rot, so we took them with us when we left. Contact was made with Mr Harold Watt of Aberdeen University Press whose father, Theodore, was advertised as a speaker at one of the meetings. He found a home for these items, donating them to the Congregational Church Archive at the City Archives.

The site was acquired in 1976, by London-based developers Minevco Ltd and ambitious plans were announced. An interesting development around the famous spire was projected with a shopping arcade, restaurant, penthouse flats and offices. An objection was made by Aberdeen Civic Society which at that time regarded anything of Archibald Simpson's as sacrosanct. The project was scrapped, much to the annoyance of the town planners who had thought the proposal as the ideal solution to a difficult site.

To treat the site as a whole was the best idea, and the Aberdeen architects, Mackie Ramsay Taylor produced a stunning, if slightly overpowering plan, which alas never materialised in reality. Division became an option as the differing condition of the Kirks became clearly apparent. East and Belmont was still relatively intact and by the early 1980s, was converted into Simpson's Bar, in memory of the architect, with outside seating near the Belmont Street corner. It was later renamed the Triple Kirks, though the interior bears little trace of its ecclesiastical origins. The top floor, a long gallery with a carved ornate ceiling, was more interesting. By 1982, enterprising plans had been drawn up for it, as the North-east's film theatre. It was to be managed jointly by the Aberdeen Art Gallery and the Scottish

'. . . a stunning if slightly overpowering plan.'

The fine bartizans of the former Belmont Congregational Church, later St Nicholas, now The Priory.

Film Council who were expected to give financial support and the project was due to come into Aberdeen City's financial estimates (1983–1984). A lift had already been installed to take the disabled to the top floor. This plan fell through at a late date but eventually the upper floor became Citymoves Dance Agency, a dance and exercise venue with a variety of classes on offer.

Albion and St Paul's, which had lain empty several years longer than East and Belmont, was deteriorating rapidly and would prove a problem, exacerbated by its virtual disappearance at the hands of the town planners. Only three shored up walls were allowed to remain, a doubtful decision to make the site more attractive than a dilapidated ruin. Minevco had leased much of the site to Barratt Commercials under an agreement requiring Barratt to develop the site for office use. The long night of planning applications was now in full swing. Five-storey office blocks with parking below . . . six-storey office blocks . . . seven storeys . . . My list takes up two A4 pages of close typing. Between August 1981 and July 1993 for example, there were seven major planning applications – three grants of outline planning permission, two grants of conditional planning permission, one appeal against refusal of planning permission, one grant of conditional listed building consent. And so on.

The brick spire remained. Sir George Younger, Secretary of State for Scotland, had complicated the scene by issuing a diktat that it must be retained. But Secretaries of State don't single-handedly make the law, and listed building consent including demolition of the spire could still have been applied for. Minevco were now seeking to terminate the lease in order to progress their own development. Litigation between Minevco and Barratts ensued, accompanied by a marked lack of interest from potential tenants.

In 1997 Grampian Enterprise, with a brief to promote business in the area and with substantial funds to offer, tried, literally, to get something off the ground. A development plan retaining the spire was drawn up by the William Cowie Partnership, as a six-storey office block with underground parking for 120 vehicles. That was never proceeded with. In March 2000 plans by Esson Properties for office accommodation for 300 on five floors,

*The Spire remains.*

plus basement floors with parking for 100 cars, was approved by the City Council. The spire would be integrated into a full-height glass atrium floodlit at night, which sounded quite exciting. Redevelopment would take up to two years. I can still recall a press photo of the Essons, father and son staring defiantly into the future with, I think, their plans in their hands. This did not proceed.

In June 2003 the local press reported that the Kirks could be transformed into a family history and architectural heritage centre, as part of a £1 billion revamp of the city centre. Esson Properties still intended to develop the site. Room might be available for an art centre. By 2004 Esson Properties were to survey the building – presumably the three walls – and assess potential costs of an office conversion. The following year, after the survey, demolition emerged as an option. Esson hoped to build sixty flats on the cleared site though it was not economically viable to incorporate the spire and its tower into this proposed development. In June 2006 Historic Scotland was to meet with owners to discuss the future of the Kirks. Nothing came of that either.

In April 2008 it was announced that the Stewart Milne Group had bought the property, apparently stepping fearlessly into the chasm. They would seek permission for restoration and conversion into offices: 'Triple Kirks will provide a unique office environment in the very heart of the city with superb views over Union Terrace Gardens.' An external inspection revealed the three remaining walls to the north-east and west, propped up with scaffolding and the brick steeple in a detached and vulnerable condition. That the site was threatened by accelerated deterioration came as no surprise. In June 2009 it was announced that Milne was to lodge a planning application later in the year. Over a year later, in September 2010, it was announced that a plan to convert the building into new city offices was to be lodged within weeks. The firm of Halliday Fraser Munro, Chartered Architects, Planning Consultants and Project Managers, was to be architect/agent for the Milne Group. Eventually, in March 2011, detailed planning permission was given for the erection of a £40 million office development and associated car parking, including the removal of the walls of the existing North Kirk and the retention of and restoration of the existing brick spire. This would come as bad news for the Queen Street

*The dome of the Academy (formerly the Central School) from the ruinous Triple Kirks.*

Church, still known to many by its old name, the North Kirk, which is some distance away, and whose walls appear perfectly sound.

In August 2011 a detailed application from the Milne Group was conditionally approved by Aberdeen City Council. The site location was given as 'Triple Kirk, former North and East Kirk 67–71 Schoolhill,' even though no such place exists. Apart from the North Kirk never being one of the Triples, the fabric of the East Kirk, later East and Belmont, now forms part of the Triple Kirks Bar. However the builders are not alone in their confusion. The Buildings at Risk in Scotland Register also refers to the interloper: 'Only here the walls of the North Kirk survive,' it notes.

This latest design for the Kirks did not prove popular and the eventual planning permission was not unanimous. The vote of the development management sub-committee was seven to four in favour of going ahead. The Vice-Convener John Corall spoke for many when he said the design would damage the historic quality of the area: 'I think the vast majority of citizens will be disappointed if it goes ahead in its present form.' Writers

*'A huge architectural blot on the landscape.' Artist's impression of plans for 'The Point'.*

to the press described the plan as looking like 'a microwave oven dropped from a far height,' and, 'another huge architectural blot on the landscape.' Aberdeen Civic Society Newsletter described the proposal as one of the least sympathetic, if not the worst produced so far:

> The building is large, bulky, encloses rather than incorporates the spire and is out of scale and character with the spire and the whole rear elevation of Belmont Street. It would also intrude on the views of the War Memorial from Union Terrace to the grave detriment of the character of this important conservation area.

This is a place where the gothic of the turrets, spires, towers and indeed, bartizans of Belmont Street blend with eastern promise of the domes of the Public Library, St Mark's, Woolmanhill Hospital, the War Memorial and the Academy, formerly the Central School in Schoolhill. No attempt had been made to attune the redeveloped Triple Kirks to the subdued exoticism of the neighbourhood. From the architect's drawings it appears as a suitable candidate for the Carbuncle Cup. Unusually, there was very little publicity about this particular proposal. Perhaps there was an understanding in the backwaters of power that protest was not to be encouraged. The Triple Kirks problem had been around for years and the planners were desperate to see the back of it, or so the story went.

The site itself is a small and difficult one and it had been suggested in the early days of the abandonment that a good solution would be to restore the Triple Kirks to their original state (as in the Wallace-in-Winter photograph opposite), and develop them as a much needed 'overflow' for Aberdeen Art Gallery. That still seems a good idea. However, in 2013 the property developers Dandara, relatively new to the North-east and clearly full of optimism, acquired the plans and the sad wreck of the spire from the Stewart Milne Group for an estimated £4 million. That August they announced a proposed investment of £20 million in providing seven storeys of open-plan office space. The structure was to be called The Point, though The Spire might have been more appropriate. 'We are proud to have acquired one of the city's true architectural jewels,' announced Dandara's managing

*A wintery Wallace hails the Triple Kirks in all their glory.*

director in Aberdeen. Work on this latest phase of the Triple Kirks saga began in the summer of 2014 but by late March 2015, with the supply of office accommodation outstripping demand, Dandara sought planning permission to switch to student accommodation.

At the end of its days, the Triple Kirks looked more like a campanile, a free-standing bell tower. It still dominated its neighbours on the rear elevation of the west side of Belmont Street, the 'Backs' of Belmont. Conversely, the 'Backs' have improved over the years. Our illustration from the 1960s on page 156 shows untidy 'Backs' as they were then and an artist's impression as to how they could look. We have virtually achieved that artist's impression.

By the later nineteenth century Betjeman's 'parade of turrets, towers and spires,' not to mention bartizans, had appeared, and was marching shoulder to shoulder with the rears of the fine eighteenth-century houses of Belmont Street and there was considerable pride in the view. In time, however, the Denburnside translated into the Denburn Road, a narrow, awkward sort of street, though still following the old route, vanishing downhill from

# UNION TERRACE GARDENS

*'The Backs of Belmont' – the rear elevation of Belmont Street in the 1960s.*

*An artist's impression of 'The Backs' from Union Terrace Gardens. In the second row are the white tower and pinnacles of John Smith's South Church and left rear, the dome of the 'Academy' shopping mall, formerly the Central School.*

# TURRETS, TOWERS AND DUAL CARRIAGEWAY

*Denburn Road. The original West Free Kirk (Albion and St Paul's) towers above.*

Woolmanhill at one end, passing under the Denburn Viaduct and fizzling out at the Green at the other. The Denburn Road was not a thriving area for beautiful gardens. The road attracted, for the most part, ugly huts and commercial buildings though it did have a curious parking area that had been a children's playground at one time with an odd little well at the back. The Denburn Road had an odd relationship with Belmont Street above. Some buildings were peculiar to one street, some to the other. Some backed up against each other. All were blackened by soot from the steam engines of the neighbouring railway.

Rescue came in the unlikely form of the Denburn dual carriageway, the relevant section of which was built in 1992. The Denburn Road was transplanted and levelled and the Denburn culvert realigned. The 'Backs' were opened up and unsightly buildings banished. The current view from Union Bridge shows that the view may not be perfect, but it is very good.

During the recent years of 'warfare', one fairly constant activity of the proponents of the City Garden Scheme was to organise a stream of supporters

# UNION TERRACE GARDENS

*The Denburn Valley railway pre-1890. In the Gardens new bandstand has pride of place and James Forbes Beattie's plan is being tentatively followed with a sprinkling of flower-beds. The iron footbridge is in situ. The railtrack has been widened to the detriment of Denburn Road. The area behind the footbridge is not yet finished nor is the amphitheatre built. Blacks Buildings dominate the rear of the scene with the Royal Infirmary, Woolmanhill, looming behind.*

*The railway beside Union Terrace Gardens in the late 1930s. The Trades Hall/Belmont Cinema is roughly central, rear.*

# TURRETS, TOWERS AND DUAL CARRIAGEWAY

*The railway in 1952.*

*Looking rather elegant, the much maligned dual carriageway and railway in 2014. A diesel leaves for Inverness. The blot on the landscape is the Denburn high-rise flats.*

to stand at Union Terrace Gardens and pose for the local press while they attacked the Denburn dual carriageway and the adjoining railway for being unsightly and intrusive. The determination to cover them was strong. But it is not unheard of to have railways running through towns and cities to reach their termini, nor is it unusual to find a dual carriageway in an urban setting. The technical appraisal for the redevelopment of Union Terrace Gardens, which was prepared for Halliday Fraser Munro in 2009 by Martha Schwartz Partners and Davis Langdon, states: 'The few diesel trains which go through the park today still form a noisy polluting intrusion.' They don't go through the park and never did, only alongside, and the old tradition of waving to the train from the Gardens, with the passengers waving back continues. It is the most attractive, stress-free entrance to the city. There are already essential tunnels at Hutcheon Street – Maberly Street and Woolmanhill, seconds away, up the track. Why condemn passengers to a non-essential third tunnel when they could be admiring green grass, bright flowers and a canopy of trees? The railway and dual carriageway run at the original level of the town, below Union Street. To be able to see them at all it is necessary to stand on Union Bridge and look down to discover that the Inverness line is not heavily used, while the dual carriageway is often an oasis of peace and calm, interrupted by the occasional car.

One of the earliest supporters of the City Garden Scheme was football 'legend' Sir Alex Ferguson, who was happy to stand at Union Terrace Gardens and denounce the road and railway. Sir Alex said, 'By raising the underused gardens and covering over the eyesore of the dual carriageway and railway, Aberdeen can reclaim its former glory and enter the premiership of European cities.' In fact, the road is quite a fine piece of civil engineering and the railway has grown more attractive over the years, as our photographs show.

CHAPTER ELEVEN

# THE GARDENS, MOSTLY IN THE TWENTIETH CENTURY

*Early days in the north end of the Gardens, c.1900.*

One of the earliest photographs of the recently completed north end, taken around 1900, shows Union Terrace Gardens looking rather stark, but there is promise. It appears to be a cold day, but there is a scattering of customers. A flower-bed in the shape of a star is perceived behind the splendidly oriental-looking bandstand which was painted every other year for much of its life and survived until the late thirties. The star would presently be replaced by the magnificent city crest. Another flower-bed takes shape over to the left and there are several jardinières scattered around. They are in use to this day. The paths are ample, in the style of the designer James Forbes Beattie, though he had not lived to see the north end rescued from housing. There is a glimpse of the handsome tri-coloured granite Denburn Viaduct on the right, whose left-hand arch is the north access to the Gardens. Beside the Viaduct, stairs lead down into the Gardens with the dome of Woolmanhill Hospital looming dimly behind. A path takes one from the upper to the lower stairs which, centrally placed within

161

# UNION TERRACE GARDENS

*His Majesty's Theatre appeared on the scene in 1906. The square tower of Schoolhill Station can be seen above the left-hand arch of the Viaduct.*

the newly created amphitheatre, is a feature in itself. Up on Rosemount Viaduct, the Public Library on the left is not yet extended, and the South Free Kirk (St Mark's) with William Wallace in front, masquerade as a part of the Gardens. H M Theatre would not be built for another six years so we have a rare sight of the handsome, east-facing elevation of the South Free, or South United Free as it became in 1900. At the foot of the central star is the Corbie Well, moved to this position after the creation of the north end, and embellished with a new granite well-head. Robert Anderson in *Aberdeen in Bygone Days*, 1910 wrote:

> It has been adorned with a curious agglomeration of civic relics – one of the pyramidal lampposts of the old Bow Brig, the weathercock of the former steeple of St Nicholas Church and a bit of the famous bell, Old Lowrie, which fell during the fire of 1874 which destroyed

the steeple and the East Church. They were placed in their present position by the late Mr Alexander Walker LLD in 1898.

One suspects that even the Links and Parks Committee might have shrunk from banning the bric-a-brac collected by so important a person as Dr Walker. The keeper of the Victoria Park, Robert Walker, who had taken Union Terrace Gardens under his wing, was congratulated by the Committee on the state of the Gardens, in spite of the state of the Corbie Well with its civic overspill.

Fearful that the Gardens' lack of acreage, coupled with its accessibility, might cause it to be quickly submerged by well-meaning donations, the Links and Parks Committee normally adopted the strictest of approaches to 'park furniture', preferring to let its handsome urns, robust granite staircases and stylish balustrading beautify the park, and at the same time to be useful

*This photograph shows the distinctive stonework of the stairs and the understated yet appropriate style of the garden furniture – jardinière, railings, seats. The War Memorial provides an impressive backdrop.*

and integral. So Aberdonians may have been surprised to find the statue of a Yankee soldier on sentry duty at the north end one day, in military cape, forage cap and cartridge pouch. It had been presented to the city and erected there by Messrs Morgan & Carnie, Sculptors (granite monumental masons) of the Clayhills, the industrial enclave where Portland Street now stands. The firm had been commissioned to produce a memorial for the American state of Wisconsin to honour those who fought for the Union in the Civil War (1861–1865). Carved in Dyce granite, the soldier was a fine piece of work, which had been much admired in the showroom. Apparently this figure had met with an accident, so reported the *Aberdeen Journal*, and another had to be substituted. The facts are vague. Whatever had happened, a granite statue of a Yankee soldier appeared in the Gardens one morning in April 1893. Morgan & Carnie were ordered by a furious Links and Parks Committee to remove the statue forthwith. Equally annoyed, the granite merchants replied to Baillie Tulloch, the Committee's chairman, expressing 'considerable surprise.' They understood the statue had been accepted and Mr Robert Walker was to arrange for its erection. The answer was that the statue had been erected without the Links and Parks Committee or any Town House official being consulted. The Committee could not allow it: 'It might form an awkward precedent.'

Morgan & Carnie might have been unaware of the fate, some three years earlier, of the obelisk in memory of the distinguished army surgeon and Lord Rector of Marischal College, Sir James McGrigor (1778–1851), constructed of pink Peterhead granite. Designed by the artist James Giles in association with the architect RG Ellis, it had been erected in the College quadrangle, but was now getting in the way of work on Marshall Mackenzie's dazzling new frontage. Sir James' obelisk had to seek a new billet. One might have thought that this would have been a suitable offering for the Gardens, but no. Permission refused. Perhaps it was a question of weight again. The Duthie Park eventually provided a suitable resting place where the obelisk, looking across to the Dee, has always seemed very much at home.

Then there was the affair of the unique fountain, made of fourteen different types of granite and presented to the citizens of Aberdeen by the

# THE GARDENS, MOSTLY IN THE TWENTIETH CENTURY

Granite Polishers and Masters Builders of Aberdeen. In 1876 a fountain, described as above, was to be erected in Union Terrace Gardens. An interesting report was published in the *Aberdeen Journal* of 25 April 1878 when work on the Gardens was approaching completion:

> About 30 yards south from the resting place of the Bow Brig the summit of a shoulder of the hill has been levelled in the line of the walk which skirts the side of Union Terrace, and a broad gravelled platform has been formed. Here it is proposed to erect the fountain which the master masons of the city intend to place in the grounds. [A detailed description of the fountain follows.] The level ground on which the fountain is to be erected will also be used as a bandstand and seats will be arranged round the platform which stands 36 feet from the street wall.

Instead this fountain materialised in the Victoria Park which had opened in 1871, and where it remains to this day. No one had told Charles Mann, for in his (undated) advertisement for the Grand Hotel the Victoria Park Fountain is there, in Union Terrace Gardens, large as life, to the left of the bandstand, with one of the urns between them. Was Mann merely anticipating the fountain's arrival when the advertisement was being

*The fountain in the Victoria Park.*

# UNION TERRACE GARDENS

*The master masons' fountain in Union Terrace Gardens as shown in the Grand Hotel advertisement.*

prepared although it never actually came to Union Terrace Gardens? Or was it taken to the Victoria Park after it proved unsuitable for the Gardens, perhaps, when together with the bandstand, it was too heavy for the ground?

We do know that the Links and Parks Committee ran the Gardens very firmly. It was a popular venue for meeting relatives and for group photographs but for the latter, permission had to be granted first. In March 1892, an epoch-making event took place. The City's Cleansing Committee was erecting public lavatories in various districts of the city, and Union Terrace was on the list. Permission to build the toilets, originally granted in the 1890s, had a difficult passage in the council chamber, eventually scraping through. At first the Rosemount Viaduct end was favoured, but in view of the crowds coming to the Gardens it seemed only sensible to locate conveniences in their vicinity. An underground lavatory for gentlemen was

# THE GARDENS, MOSTLY IN THE TWENTIETH CENTURY

*The souvenir photograph of the Conference of Scottish Savings Workers at Aberdeen 18–19 June, 1920. The photographer was D Milne, 158 King Street, Aberdeen.*

constructed at the south end of Union Terrace, at the junction with Union Street. It was located in the cavernous space under the statue of Prince Albert, with access via a flight of stone stairs on the south side of the main entrance, matching the staircase on the north side which takes one into the Gardens and to the Ladies'. The toilets were innovative and with their enrichment of stained glass, considered over the top by many councillors at a time when Gents' were primitive affairs, and Ladies' did not exist.

The Gents' were ornate, controversial and, at a cost of £990, expensive. There were originally eleven urinals, later increased to twenty-three, presumably by popular demand. They were made by Doulton (soon to be Royal) of Lambeth and Paisley. The decorative wall tiles were glazed in rich green bands beneath a moulded dado, and ornate mounded tiles formed a cornice at the wallhead around the blocks of toilet cubicles. When the Prince Albert statue was replaced at street level by the much heavier Edward VII and his entourage in 1914, a pillar, introduced to support the roof, was camouflaged in the matching green glazed tiles. On the floor there were

The Gents' toilets when in use, opposite. Note the sturdy doors, top left. The handsome stained-glass window helps to provide light. The tiles are mid-green, the ivy dark green.

# THE GARDENS, MOSTLY IN THE TWENTIETH CENTURY

beige Granolite tiles in a mosaic pattern, with a broad Greek key border. The ceiling tiles were pale cream.

Daylight was provided from the pavement of Union Street above by multi-paned rectangular glass Lenscrete skylights. Windows with upper panes of stained glass offered a little more light. These can be seen from the outside at the extreme south end of the Gardens, beside Union Bridge, piercing the vast outer semi-circular granite wall of the Gents'. It is in rock-faced ashlar – as is much of the stone work in the Gardens – and quite spectacular, but a deep shade of green as I write. It only needs a good scrub to further transform this end of the Gardens, where a young rhododendron walk is coming along.

*The semicircular rock-faced granite wall at the south end of the Gardens. A young Rhododendron walk is coming on below.*

*The turntable, bottom centre in sunlight, looks much better these days when cleared of rubbish. King Edward VII stands erect above the Gents' toilets.*

The Ladies' did not share the cavernous block with the Gents', nor did they have the same décor. They were reached by the stairway of the main entrance, in the opposite direction from the Gents'. They were modestly tucked out of sight within the first arch of that long granite-faced arcade that runs the length of the Gardens. In this era Gents' alone was the norm. Having a Ladies' was a breakthrough, a step towards equality, recognition that ladies too might require to use the facilities when out and about. A gate was positioned to give access when the Gardens themselves were closed. A faded Art Deco fanlight at the entrance, reminiscent of the Paris Metro and still visible, but only just, reads 'Ladies". Their tiling was in dusky pink and warm brown in an Art Nouveau design with stylised flowers reminiscent of Charles Rennie Mackintosh. There was a row of probably six toilets, wash-hand-basins and an attendant's room. The Ladies' had the same rectangular panels in the roof containing small panes of reinforced glass which provided some light. You could hear high heels clicking and clacking over them, above. There was always a special carbolicky smell in the Ladies', which opened quite early in the morning. They were popular, pristine, well run and I remember the attendant as pleasant but firm. Unfortunately, over the years the City Council allowed these listed toilets to fall into a state of neglect. I once saw a crass, unsuitable replacement sink being plumbed in.

Apart from the loss of a part of the heritage, the city centre is, at time of writing, bereft of public toilets, given that those in Upperkirkgate have been closed off, and those in the Music Hall are only open to customers of the café there. A group of us tried to have the toilets open for Doors Open Day in 2012 only to be met by official stalling and cries that 'Health and Safety' would not allow it. Wildly different estimates have been given for reinstatement, one, from a councillor, as high as £2.5 million, which sounds like a tactic to discourage action. Some structural work will be necessary in the Gents' though King Edward VII does not appear to have fallen through the pavement yet – but providing that the Council still employs engineers, plumbers, joiners and painters or knows someone who does, much could be done 'in house'.

Prior to closure, RCAHMS (Royal Commission on the Ancient and Historic Monuments of Scotland) reported that the toilets stood below the statue of King George VI, but after this unpromising start, it got better: 'At the time of this survey, this facility was threatened with closure, and despite still being in use was in a very poor condition. However, its original splendour was still very evident, and many of its fittings and much of its decor were comparable to those at Rothesay Pier's gentlemen's toilets.' These are now advertised as 'Rothesay's World Class Toilets . . . the most impressive surviving late Victorian public convenience in Scotland if not Britain.' Splendid though they are, they are neither as big nor as grand nor as expensive as the original Union Terrace Gardens toilets were, yet are a major holiday attraction for Bute. I have perhaps spent too much time in the toilets, but their deterioration and closure, in 2000, is one of Aberdeen's minor tragedies. It would not take a great deal to get the Ladies' at least up and running again.

The park furniture of Union Terrace Gardens was usually of a more modest variety than exotic toilets, but in 1931 it did receive an unusual lodger, Sheriff Thomson's Arch. In 1673 Andrew Thomson, advocate in Aberdeen and Sheriff-Depute, originally erected this arched gateway to his house at No. 21 Guestrow and it bears the initials A T 1673 AD, those of

# UNION TERRACE GARDENS

*Sheriff Thomson's Arch in the Guestrow, its original site.*

*A glimpse of the Thomson Arch at the start of the Rose Walk. A stage has been set up in the amphitheatre for an open-air performance.*

## THE GARDENS, MOSTLY IN THE TWENTIETH CENTURY

*The Rose Walk, centre, from the south. The arch is at the far end.*

the Sheriff and his wife Agnes Divie. During the slum clearance of 1931, the arch was considered too valuable to smash up and was taken to Union Terrace Gardens where it stood at the north end of the Rose Walk. In 1965 it was returned to a spot close to its original site, beside the entrance to the newly restored Provost Skene's House. But the Archway does not rest in peace. At time of writing, the firm involved in the Marischal Square development want rid of it and in 2014 sought to have it moved again. Perhaps a return to the Gardens might be considered.

In May 1936 new open-air draughtsboards were provided for Union Terrace Gardens by the Town Council on the initiative of the local draughts club. Lord Provost Watt performed the opening ceremony and after declaring the boards ready for customers, made the first move in front of a large gathering of enthusiasts. Men playing draughts – you rarely saw women – became an enduring image of the Gardens.

*A game of draughts in progress while spectators relax.*

There was always something happening in the amphitheatre in the summertime. Pipe bands and Highland dancers were popular as were ballroom dancing and fashion shows. And I can distinctly remember scary Punch and Judy shows. Union Terrace Gardens were a popular backdrop for publicity shots with actors performing at H M Theatre across the road.

The Gardens had always been beautifully kept, but in the early 1980s, they began to show signs of decline. Comparison was inevitably made with

# THE GARDENS, MOSTLY IN THE TWENTIETH CENTURY

*Highland Dancing in the amphitheatre.*

the Duthie Park. It was felt that money had been poured into the Winter Gardens for example, during the years when David Welch was Links and Parks supremo. Even during the golden era of 'Britain in Bloom', Union Terrace Gardens was something of a City Centre Cinderella. There were other criticisms, that the grass needed returfing, the draughts had vanished, and though the city crest made its annual appearance, what had happened to its smaller companions which were redesigned annually to mark various local anniversaries? The floral creations in their honour were always works of art. Now all that remained were ghostly marks in the turf. And where was the floral clock? Some cynics voiced the opinion that the Gardens were being run down, in order to appear ripe for development.

Worse still, the arches had become the haunt of glue-sniffers, alcoholics and the like and many people, particularly women, did not wish to go down to the Gardens any more.

*The Bandstand.*

Chapter Twelve

# 'THE BEST LAID SCHEMES OF MICE AND MEN . . .'

Schemes for altering, converting, improving, covering and filling-in have buzzed round Union Terrace Gardens like bees round a honey pot if not since time immemorial, at least since the days of Robert Gordon's Technical College a stone's throw away in Schoolhill. Students of architecture there could be given the challenging task of working out innovatory and ground-breaking plans for the Gardens, without the responsibility of having to put them into action. It was a tradition that survived the move to Garthdee and at least some versions had elegant bridges linking the Gardens with Belmont Street and the city centre.

Several factors in the 1980s: an apparent decline in the husbandry of the Gardens, the increasing value of the ground they occupied and the shortage of city centre parking stimulated a further onslaught of plans. All included raising the Gardens to create car parking below, and some the 'added bonus' that the Inverness railway line and an upgraded Denburn Road would be hidden from view. One of the most ambitious was a £20 million scheme of 1984 by Albyn Design Associates, which as well as raising the level to contain three floors of parking, would create luxury town houses, flats, patios, balconies, shops, offices, a four-star hotel on Rosemount Viaduct, a civic square at Union Bridge with the Edward VII group and the panels from the Bridge as centre pieces. The existing trees, the rookery and balustrades would be retained and an amphitheatre, presumably unaware that there was one there already, would be built. Discussions with a major hotel group, house builders and national retailers were underway, not to mention National Car Parks – always a doleful thought. Union Street from Union Bridge to the Castlegate would be pedestrianised, the derelict buildings on Denburn Road would be screened and it would take four years to complete. In retrospect it seemed good value for £20 million.

## UNION TERRACE GARDENS

There was opposition, of course. A protest group from Aberdeen University and RGIT felt the plan unnecessary. It would cause traffic congestion and destroy a unique part of Aberdeen. A petition started by a certain geologist, Mike Shepherd, against any redevelopment of Union Terrace Gardens quickly gained signatories. 'There has been a tremendous response and I have been amazed,' he told the press. In due course the scheme was rejected by Aberdeen City District Planning Committee who also envisaged issuing a specific edict that they would not favour any major structural development on Union Terrace Gardens.

In August 1985, however, Aberdeen Chamber of Commerce, at that time, I think, still in Union Terrace, launched a petition in favour of the development of the Gardens. Their proposals included raising them to the

*Union Terrace Gardens as a parking lot.*

level of the Terrace and inserting a three-floor car park below. In response, the City Planning Committee did issue their specific edict that they would not favour any major structural development of the Gardens. The Chamber called this premature. And, adopting an altruistic stance, they argued that an 'appropriate development on this site is essential for the well-being of the community' and suggested the project 'should be the subject of an architectural competition.' Nothing came of that.

By early 1987 another scheme for 'this famous city centre beauty spot' was underway, proposed by Condor Projects (Scotland) and National Car Parks: a multi-storey car park topped by new terraced gardens nearer street level. Again the proposal was rejected, with Councillor David Clyne initiating a petition against it, leading the opposition, and successfully proposing a motion under which the majority of mature trees would be protected 'for all time' by a tree preservation order.

A report entitled *Aberdeen Beyond 2000*, undated, but probably 1987, was launched by members of the business community, convinced that if their suggestions were acted on, the city's prosperity would be ensured well into the twenty-first century. The name of Ian Wood, the enterprising head of the family-owned, oil-related company, tops the list of supporting firms. He expressed angst about the city's future prosperity. One solution in the report was to exploit the Green's underused potential by turning it into a car park, another, and it will come as no surprise, was to bring Union Terrace Gardens, described as 'a waste of space', up to street level.

The crusade to alter the Gardens continued. In September 1990 Susan Chisholm wrote to the press:

> It was with huge dismay that I listened to Councilor Bob Middleton on Radio Aberdeen resurrecting the dreadful old scheme to 'raise' Union Terrace Gardens and form a huge piazza. This, he suggests, would bring us in line with most other leading European cities. Enough has been done to destroy and deface Aberdeen.

The piazza didn't happen, but by March 1992 Aberdeen City Centre Project, a partnership of Aberdeen District and Grampian Regional

# UNION TERRACE GARDENS

Aberdeen Beyond 2000 *showed a photograph of a surfer and advised that the Beach was a ten-minute walk from the city centre. Leopard Magazine published a cartoon by Jane Ancona in July 1987, of the great and the good of the day setting off on their ten-minute walk for a spot of surfing. Lord Provost Henry E Rae is the starter. Note balustrades!*

Councils, Scottish Homes and Grampian Enterprise, presented a new multi-million-pound scheme. The latter was the new kid on the block, the local arm of Scottish Enterprise, or more formally a Non-Departmental Public Body, with a brief to encourage industry and a budget to go with it. A new city square and terrace overlooking the Gardens was proposed with a stepped terrace from Union Street. Denburn Road to become was a dual carriageway. There would be parking for 840 cars in two tiers below street level and potential for a 200,000 square feet development 'which could become the new cultural, civic and business focus of the city.'

In July of that year, Grampian Enterprise Ltd (GEL) presented to district councillors their new multi-million pound version of the scheme (though still at the 'conceptual' stage) to revitalise the city. It appears to have been a version of the previous scheme. It revealed ambitous plans to deck over the railway line and the proposed Denburn dual carriageway. 'Foundation supports [piles] for the decking have already been included in the Denburn Road works at a cost of over £1 million paid for by Scottish Enterprise and

'THE BEST LAID SCHEMES OF MICE AND MEN...'

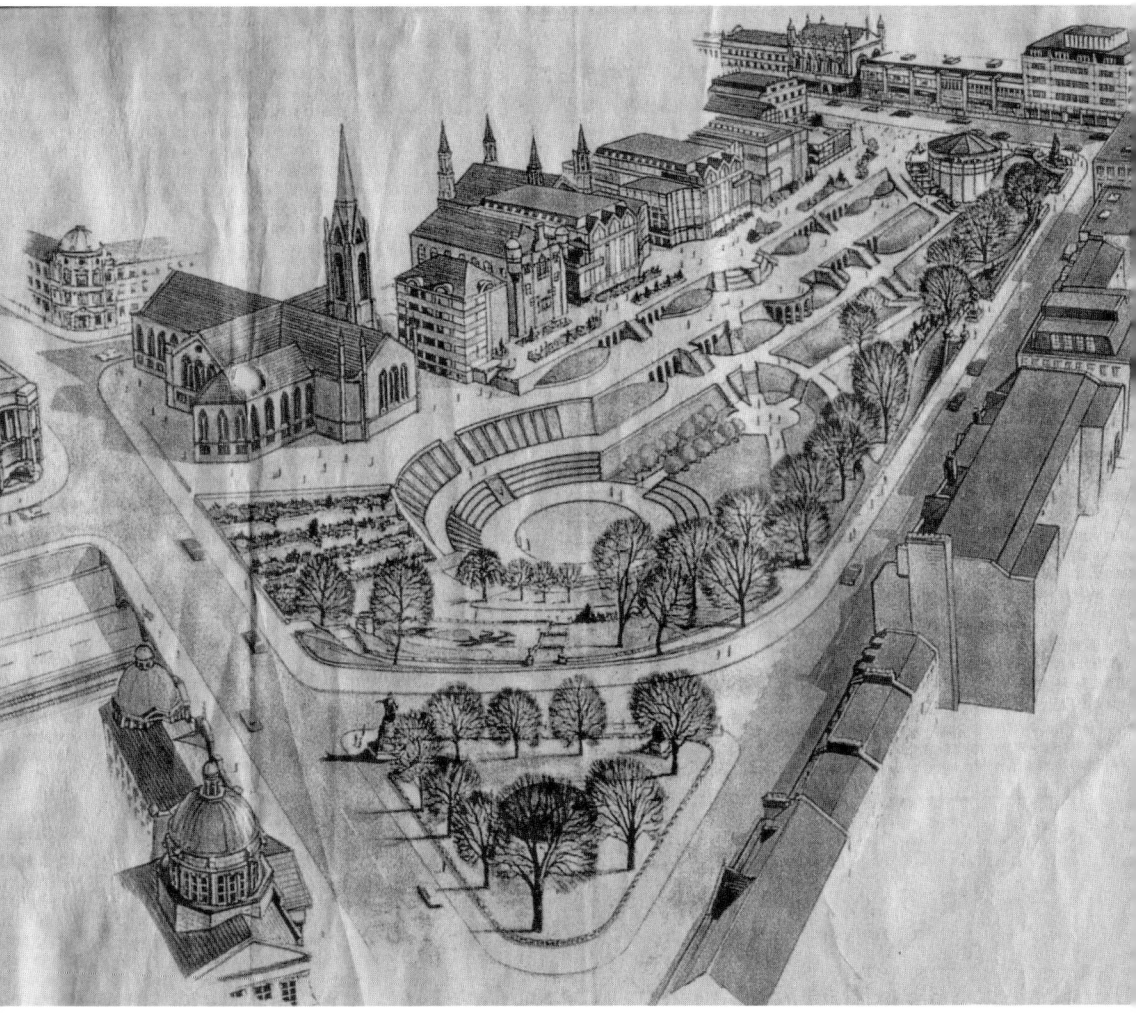

*The scheme of July 1992 by Grampain Enterprise Ltd.*

Grampian Enterprise,' the report read. The brilliance of the foresight in proposing to lay these foundations, intended at some point to carry decking to allow an extension of the scheme, was extolled in every article on the scheme. This newly available area would have a stepped concourse with shops and offices, and was being hailed as one of the biggest and costliest projects ever undertaken in the city centre. Norman Marr, Head of Planning for Kincardine Deeside wrote to the press to point out that this scheme, 'on which large sums of money have already been spent on foundations, without any planning permission or opportunity for pubic comment, has not been authorised by the citizens of Aberdeen.' The Denburn Road, which had begun life as the gravel walk, was dualled between 1993 and 1994 at a cost of £16 million. The Denburn Viaduct seamlessly gained a fourth arch to take the dual carriageway and a part of the Denburn culvert was realigned. As for the illegal decking scheme, it never got off the ground and the piles cannot now be located.

At the beginning of 1994, a £50 million plan produced by the Regional and District Councils and Grampian Enterprise was of the 'here today, gone tomorrow' variety. The basic principle behind the design was that Union Bridge should be preserved. This did not impress a potential developer who wanted the Bridge covered over and made flush with Union Street. The parking offered was deemed inadequate and the restricted access from Union Street did not impress. In other words, it lacked 'commercial viability'.

Next came the era of the Millennium schemes. In 1995 a £67 million plan was turned down by the Millennium Commission as not economically viable. It had proposed multi-decking on the east side of the Valley, housing a two-tier car park. A variety of shapes were stuck along the top tier of the model, representing shops and office blocks, blotting out the fine rear elevations of Belmont Street and virtually overwhelming the Gardens. The Commission advised a trimming back, presumably on costs as well as bulk, before re-submission. A joint bid to the Millennium Commission, a second submission by Aberdeen City Council and Grampian Enterprise Ltd was launched in November 1996 at a press conference in the Town House: 'This exciting application aims to transform Union Terrace Gardens into the new heart of Aberdeen and is set to create hundreds of jobs in the city,' read the hand-out. An extension of the existing Gardens would be built above the railway and dual carriageway with civic space for exhibitions, festival offices, tourist information, restaurants, shops, amenity areas and two urban squares (which as far as I could make out from the plan were proposed for two Belmont Street back gardens). The rejuvenation of Union Terrace Gardens and the potential development of the Triple Kirks site were also to be undertaken. I seem to recall that it was one of those cases where

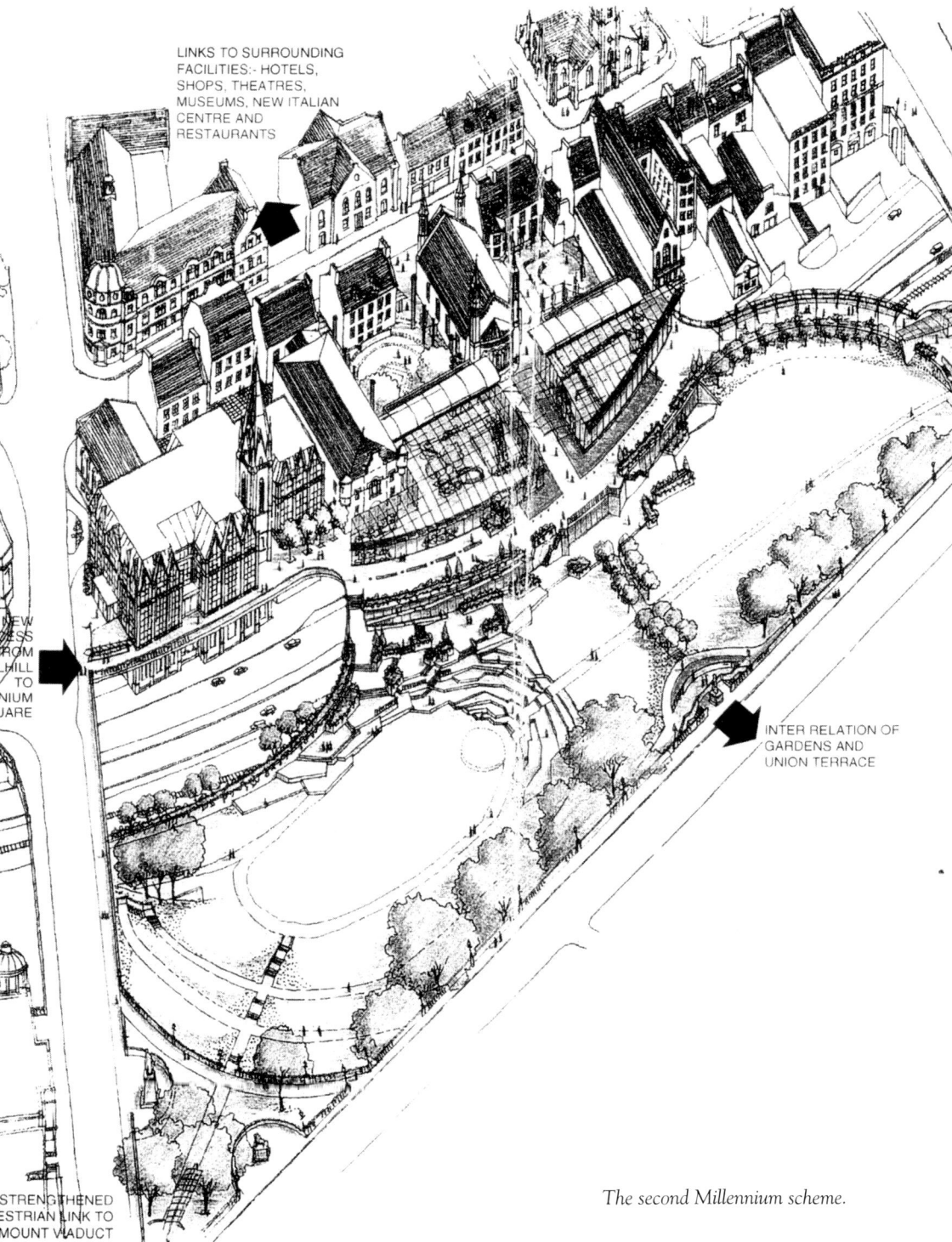

*The second Millennium scheme.*

consultation did not take place when matters were at a formative stage as it should have done. Attempts to inspect the model of the new submission at St Nicholas House were frustrated by the fact that only obsolete models were on view. The conservationist Connie Leith, who was on the same quest as myself, wrote, 'eventually even these quietly disappeared from the Council's Planning and Strategic Development Department.' The scheme was rejected on grounds that 'it was not distinctive enough.' Councillors declared themselves 'mystified' with the Millennium Commission's decision.

There was a hiatus for some time, then on 27 February 2008, the Scottish Government approved funding for a Contemporary Arts Centre for a local group, Peacock Visual Arts. The Peacock Group of artists and printmakers had been looking for new premises for some time since the lease of their original base at Peacock's Close off the Castlegate was due to expire. They had after long length found a suitable site – Union Terrace Gardens. The publicity was brimming with confidence:

> Led by Peacock Visual Arts – Aberdeen's celebrated contemporary organisation – this landmark development will become a creative powerhouse to the North-east of Scotland. Aberdeen's historic Union Terrace Gardens will provide location for one of the most exciting cultural developments in today's Scotland . . . The Centre's artistic programme will attract some of the world's most exciting artists, and develop a truly global network out of its Aberdeen base.

And so on. Those in Aberdeen who had not heard of Peacock Visual Arts soon would. Planning permission had been granted, financial backing had come from Scottish Enterprise, the European Union, Aberdeen City Council and the Scottish Arts Council and other funding and was well on the way to completion.

Not everyone was enamoured of the idea of a contemporary arts organisation, or anything else for that matter, being built in the Gardens. In spite of promises that the centre would be tucked in beside the arches at the Union Terrace end, the illustration of their proposed headquarters showed what appeared to be large grass-covered hillocks descending from the old Corbie Heugh to the bottom of the Valley. Nevertheless, in general, a sigh of relief was heaved. It was felt that the predators of Union Terrace Gardens were finally seen off. However, it was not to be quite like that.

Chapter Thirteen

# THE BATTLE FOR UNION TERRACE GARDENS: MIKE SHEPHERD REPORTS

*I have asked Mike Shepherd to contribute a chapter on the economic aspects of the City Garden Project. This is relevant as the proposal ultimately failed due to a lack of funding and the feeble business case made for it. Mike was the first chairman of the Friends of Union Terrace Gardens and campaigned against the City Garden Project. In this capacity he closely followed the economic arguments on both sides and the text reflects this perspective. A geologist by profession, Mike has an Honours Degree in Geology and Mineralogy from Aberdeen University. In 2009 his book on Oil Field Production Geology was published by the American Association of Petroleum Geologists. DM*

In November 2008, Aberdeen's oil billionaire Sir Ian Wood surprised the people of Aberdeen when he announced at a press conference in the H M Theatre that he was prepared to allocate up to £50 million to raise Union Terrace Gardens to street level and thus create a civic square. The announcement was unexpected, not the least because Aberdeen Council had given planning permission to Peacock Visual Arts only four months previously, to build a 'centre for contemporary arts' in the park. The proposed £13.5 million building was to contain a gallery, a TV studio, a print studio, a restaurant and offices for the Peacock staff. It would also provide a base for Aberdeen City Council's Arts Development and Arts Education teams, as well as extra space for the Citymoves dance agency.

Sir Ian's £50 million was not enough to fully complete his project and he recognised this. He insisted that the proposal would only go ahead if it was backed by the people of the North-east and received significant public funding. The First Minister of the Scottish government at the time, Alex Salmond, had been present at the meeting in H M Theatre with Sir Ian Wood. The First Minister was quoted in the next day's *Evening Express*:

Such a project would have an extremely strong case of going forward to seek public funding, not just from the city council but from the Scottish Government and from the identifiable Lottery fundings, which are available for such major projects.

The same newspaper article mentioned that Scottish Enterprise had been given the task of establishing the feasibility, design and cost of the scheme.

The public reaction to the announcement was mixed. At this stage, the most clearly upset element in Aberdeen was the arts community. The scale of Sir Ian Wood's vision left no space for Peacock's contemporary arts centre as originally planned. Although Peacock Visual Arts had been given planning permission for their arts centre, they had not yet been assigned a property lease that would legally allow them to build in the park. Sir Ian Wood's proposed scheme would also compete for the same lease and only one of them could pick it up from the council. The local arts community reacted by setting up a pressure group called 'I Heart UTG', with Kate Guthrie and Fraser Denholm taking the lead. The aim of the group was to push the case for the contemporary arts centre, which they now saw as under threat. I contacted the campaigners shortly after they formed. The impression I gained was of a very enthusiastic group of committed youngsters, who were determined to persevere with their ambitious project. They had worked very hard in raising an impressive amount of money to help fund it.

Attempts were made to try and accommodate the Peacock scheme within the civic square. Documents released later showed that Scottish Enterprise had assumed that Peacock would fall in line with the larger project, and that an arts centre could be built under the Civic Square, although not in the form that Peacock had envisaged. Scottish Enterprise were so convinced that this would happen, they used £190,000 of public funds already allocated as a grant to Peacock Visual Arts to pay for the technical feasibility study for the civic square. Nevertheless, the negotiations with Peacock foundered without resolution. They did not want their new facility to be placed underground, and they told me that their main objection was that an arts centre needed to be open to plenty of natural light to be able to function properly. The artists were extremely proud of their design for the contemporary arts centre and were most reluctant to give it up. However, it proved impractical to accommodate the original Peacock design within the Civic Square proposal, as they occupied markedly different levels within the air space above Union Terrace Gardens.

The technical feasibility study for the civic square was made public in June 2009. It envisaged a three-storey steel and concrete structure built within the area of Union Terrace Gardens and, together with the railway and dual carriageway, they were all to be decked over with access to the city square at street level from four sides. The overall cost was estimated as £140 million, although various extra items of expenditure had been excluded from this total.

At this point it wasn't clear what the underground space beneath the city square would actually be used for and an admission of this was made in the technical feasibility study:

> The design process for Union Terrace Gardens will be unlike most design processes. Most conventional designs tend to start with a use, before proceeding to a site and then a brief, and finally designs to enable a scheme to be built. For Union Terrace Gardens, this will effectively be reversed. This is partly because the scheme is opportunity led, but mostly because of the scale and significance of the expected design. This scheme will be, by its very nature, more akin to designing a new street in the city, than designing a new building.

The architects behind the study made some helpful suggestions. An extensive shopping centre was unfeasible given the ongoing construction of the massive Union Square mall nearby. However, a 490-bay car park could be built on the ground floor and the upper two levels could include the arts centre, boutique shops, cafés, a heritage centre, even a hotel was suggested. The frontage at street level adjacent to Union Bridge could allow commercial building on the northern side of the Union Street crossing. The technical feasibility report was candid about an issue that would dominate the controversy about the project in the years to follow:

The difficulty in quantifying the economic gain is considerable. To describe the benefits in cultural and civic terms; and to focus on the future *raison d'être* of the City of Aberdeen will become the means of explaining the benefits. However it is very difficult to make these benefits seem tangible. Yet this is precisely what will have to be done for a proposal to succeed. It is not just that it should be popular, it is also that it should be far more than just 'value for money'. Regional and Sub-Regional benefits would have to be a 'given' since the real litmus test would have to be in terms of National and International benefits.

The controversy started to ramp up in Aberdeen. Early illustrations of what the civic square might look like at street level had failed to impress. These somewhat implausibly showed crowds of people walking happy and contented over a bleak and largely featureless expanse of square. Many saw the suggestion of car parking, shops and hotels for the concourse under the city square as the commercialisation of open green space. Later, the city square supporters would give more emphasis to the cultural benefits, such as an open-air theatre and a heritage museum.

Following the publication of the technical feasibility study, the management of the project was handed over to ACSEF (Aberdeen City and Shire Economic Future). This is an organisation set up and funded by Scottish Enterprise, Aberdeen City and Aberdeenshire councils. Largely run by local businessmen, the group was intended to provide both councils with economic advice at regional level. ACSEF has proved unpopular with those on the left wing of the political spectrum as they are seen as an unelected group that have been given control over regional economic issues, without the need to submit to a democratic audit.

ACSEF organised a public consultation on what was now described as the 'City Square Project'. Funded by the public body Scottish Enterprise, the overall cost of the consultation was £113,680. One prominent poster in a shop window in Union Street claimed that: 'Through public consultation you are now being asked if, and how, this project will go ahead.' A number of stalls were put in shopping malls and other areas around the city and shire to publicise the consultation. Focus groups were set up with local community councils to allow them to discuss the plans. This came across to me as a marketing exercise rather than a proper consultation. There was very little effort to provide any alternative arguments against the city square proposal, even though these were being vociferously voiced within Aberdeen. For example, the Peacock scheme was never mentioned.

The consultation culminated in a vote based on both a questionnaire and the key question: 'Do you support the City Square Project?' It was possible to vote by post, online or by telephone. The online voting proved quirky as the default answer to the poll was a 'Yes' on the page. A report was published later by the organisers of the poll, giving a detailed breakdown on individual voting responses together with any comments made to back up the voting choice. The numerous and obvious mismatches between the voting intention and the associated comments would appear to indicate that many taking part had inadvertently voted 'Yes' when they thought they had voted 'No'. Fraser Denholm found out from a Freedom of Information Act request that the organisers were regularly monitoring feedback from the consultation. The 'I Heart UTG' group managed to undermine the tactical advantage of being able to screen the returns by collecting a large number of 'No' votes on paper ballots and then submitting them on the last day of the poll. This proved effective.

In response to the question: 'Do you support the City Square Project?' The result was that 55% voted 'No', with 44% voting 'Yes' and 1% having spoiled their ballots. A majority of 1,270 said 'No' out of the 11,943 persons taking part. The public had clearly rejected the City Square Project.

The next three months saw ACSEF trying to wriggle out of any commitment to the poll result and to spin what had been a disastrous outcome for the City Square into something that sounded much more positive. This was not an easy task and would involve a significant degree of deftness with both fact and logic. For instance, a 55%:44% vote was labelled a split vote; the 11,943 poll count was deemed a low turnout and the numerous comments given online, many in support of the Peacock project, were taken to indicate a desire for change. And change was then assumed to be tacit support for the City Square.

The group had requested that a full Aberdeen City Council meeting on

19 May 2010 should discuss the public consultation. ACSEF minutes of the 20 April 2010 meeting mention that a press release was to be issued with ACSEF's analysis of the consultation results: 'ACSEF states that the public do want change [and] respects the fact that opinions are divided.'

On 5 May 2010, the *Scotsman* newspaper published a story with the headline: 'Reject city square at your peril, business bosses warn.' Over fifty local businessmen had written to Aberdeen Council asking them to proceed with the City Square Project, despite the result of the public consultation. Excerpts from the business letter were quoted:

> Aberdeen City Council should be very concerned about the very real damage that rejection of this £140m investment will cause to Aberdeen City's already tarnished reputation.
> Around the world, we will be known as the city which turned down a £50m private sector donation towards an ambitious and much-needed public infrastructure development at a time when other councils throughout the UK would have grasped it with open arms.
> As businesses employing 40,000 people locally with a combined turnover of £13 billion, we would like some reassurance from our city council that this opportunity will not be denied simply due to misunderstanding of the project among the public and an inability to appreciate the very real impact that high quality civic amenities and an excellent city centre can have on the regional economy.
> It is absolutely essential that the council supports this project to enable it to progress to the next stage – an international design competition. While public opinion has been divided, we believe a significant number of the silent majority have expressed a clear desire to pursue it.
> If we let this window close, the clear message will be that we do not have the ambition or the foresight to prevent a downward spiral that will see a serious decline in our economy.

The idea that not building the City Square would result in a downward spiral in the local economy could, in my opinion, at best be described as contentious – at worst, ludicrous. My view was that the patronising tone in the business letter had to be challenged and this prompted me to send the following letter to *The Press and Journal*:

> SIR – Local businessmen have asked Aberdeen City Council to go ahead with the City Square Project and to ignore the vote in the recent consultation 'due to misunderstanding of the project among the public' and an 'inability' to appreciate its impact.
>
> The message is clear: the majority of us that voted against the project are too stupid to be taken seriously. The Council should be aware that we understand the scheme only too well, which is why we rejected it. The proposal that the 'No' vote should be ignored by the Council because the public didn't understand what they were doing is an insult to the people of Aberdeen.

Council officials prepared a report for the meeting on 19 May 2010. They recommended that councillors should approve Sir Ian Wood's offer of £50 million based on the ACSEF analysis, and that the City Square Project should proceed to the next stage. Councillors at the May Council meeting then voted through this item. What the vote meant in practice was that the Council had now endorsed the City Square Project in spite of the consultation result. Several years of work lay ahead to finalise a plan and to secure funding, and once this was in place a submission could then be made for planning consent. On the assumption that this would be successful, it would now be the City Square Project that would be given the lease for Union Terrace Gardens and not the Peacock Arts Centre. Despite the Peacock artists having planning permission and much of their funding in place for their Arts Centre, the vote had effectively killed off their plans.

Unfortunately, I wasn't present at the 19 May 2010 Council meeting due to work commitments; however, I did manage to meet up with the Peacock artists later that evening at the Blackfriars pub. I hadn't expected a happy occasion and it most certainly wasn't. They had brought along a box of champagne bottles, with the intention of celebrating had the Council rejected the city square and thus allowed their arts centre to go ahead. I had turned up to offer moral support and to see if there was any fight left in the 'I Heart UTG' campaign, but there clearly wasn't. The dream had died.

A tremendous sense of outrage was evident in the city following the decision at the council meeting. This was reflected in a report issued by the Council themselves shortly afterwards. Every year, the Council carry out a citizens' panel community questionnaire, compiled with the intention of gauging public opinion on local matters, and a public report is issued analysing the responses. This is an extract from the 2010 report:

> The issue of Union Terrace Gardens arose repeatedly in the categories of 'The Council doesn't listen to or act on people's concerns' and 'Previous negative experience'. People felt that the consultation conducted on behalf of the Council had effectively been ignored, leaving many people with a sense of absolute futility and impotence. Comments reflecting this included the following strongly worded contributions:
> 'Recent events with Union Terrace Gardens [. . .] demonstrate [that] public opinion is not valued over commercial interest.'
> 'Considering the views of the Aberdeen people on the 'public consultation' regarding Union Terrace Gardens were completely ignored, it's up to you to convince me that consultation [responses] given in good faith are not a complete waste of time and money.'

ACSEF had now rebranded the City Square Project as the City Garden Project. There was much talk about winning hearts and minds in support of the scheme. I had been told that with the 'I Heart UTG' campaign out of the way, ACSEF had bargained on general public acceptance for the project. They were wrong. A group of very angry citizens found each other via the Internet and word of mouth, coming together to form a new campaign group: 'The Friends of Union Terrace Gardens'. I was made the chairman of the group. My own personal involvement in the campaign stemmed from my passion for the granite heritage of Aberdeen. Modern buildings are made of concrete almost everywhere in the world and each old building replaced with concrete leads to an erosion of the uniqueness of special cities such as Aberdeen. Union Terrace Gardens occupies a symbolic place in the geography of Aberdeen. If you keep the Gardens there, you are making a statement that heritage matters. If you replace them with a modern twenty-first-century park you are effectively stating that this gives new development the priority over the preservation of Aberdeen's heritage.

Sympathetic politicians from several parties gave us advice. A key aim was to try and keep credibility with the Aberdeen public and to avoid being marginalised in the media with the label of 'tree-hugging hippies'. The City Garden Project would have to undergo several administrative hurdles before it was ever likely to achieve planning permission. If you were savvy about council procedure, supportive politicians told us, you could throw a lot of grit into the smooth running of the procedural process.

The Friends Group announced themselves to the Aberdeen public at the start of June 2010, when at the initiative of Steve Bothwell we drove a red London bus around the centre of Aberdeen. We circled around the city centre, broadcasting the music from the film *Summer Holiday* and with a banner announcing what was effectively our first public demonstration –

a large jamboree in Union Terrace Gardens on 12 June 2010. I have fond memories of the public waving and cheering at us from the street, and several hundred supporters attended the jamboree on the day.

The City Garden Project was to come up in discussion again at the 30 June 2010 Council meeting. We would only later realise that our first act to try and impede the procedural machinery had resulted in delaying the project by ten months. Aberdeen Council allows individuals to make deputations to Council meetings. This involves making a speech to the councillors for ten minutes prior to a debate. We argued that the Council revenue budget, the budget that is used to provide services to the community, should not be used for funding any preparation work for the City Garden Project. The Chief Executive of the Council agreed with us, and it would be over a year before alternative sources of funding could be found for the project.

As the months and years passed, Council meeting after Council meeting voted to continue with the City Garden Project. Although we had managed to slow down progress, a majority of councillors supported the project every time and it took on the appearance of a juggernaut that could not be stopped no matter how hard you tried.

*Campaigner Melba Gibson outside the City Garden Design Exhibition.*

Nevertheless, there was the tricky matter of paying for the project. The £140 million nominal cost had been divided up at £70 million each for the private and public sector. Sir Ian Wood had promised £50 million and an anonymous backer had pledged another £5 million to make the private sector sum a total of £55 million. This was still £15 million short of the promised £70 million.

An unconventional idea had been proposed to raise the £70 million allocation from the public sector. The Scottish government was considering the introduction of a tax-raising scheme that is widely used in the United States. This is known as Tax Incremental Financing (TIF). The tax scheme had been designed for rust-belt cities in the US, where the local economy had collapsed. It works like this: a city council borrows money from government funds for a regeneration project within the city, and once it is built the new project makes money and is then liable for the payment of business rates. The rates are used by the city council to pay back the initial loan over a twenty-five-year period. These are rates that would not have been created had it not been for the initial investment in the first place, so the city coffers are not missing out. The TIF funding is thus intended to be self-financing. The uplift in economic activity can ideally lead to the regeneration of a city's otherwise moribund local economy. This type of scheme is not without risk, as a gross misjudgement of the business case could leave a struggling city council with large debts to service.

In January 2011, a limited company called the Aberdeen City Garden Trust (ACGT) was formed with the aim of taking the City Garden Project through the design and construction phase. The two directors identified in the company documents for the ACGT were also members of ACSEF. Questions were being asked about who would eventually own the land on the Union Terrace Gardens side of the Denburn Valley, should the City Garden Project be built. We had established that the park was Common Good land and indeed we had discovered an old legal document that stated on no account were the grounds to be used for anything other than recreational purposes. A Council official told us that Aberdeen Council would retain ownership, but would consider assigning a 125-year lease for the land.

*Street protests in the campaign to save Union Terrace Gardens.*

# UNION TERRACE GARDENS

In March 2011, money was eventually provided to finance the operational needs of the City Garden Project, as it moved forward to the planning stage. The funds came from two sources: Sir Ian Wood gave £400,000 to the ACGT, and Scottish Enterprise, who had funded the public consultation that had rejected the scheme, also gave £375,000 of public money to the company.

The money was used to organise an international design competition for the City Garden Project. A shortlist of six submissions from various architectural companies and groups were identified. A jury, with Sir Ian Wood as a prominent member, would pick the winner from amongst them. The public would be allowed to comment on the designs and the jury would take these comments into account while making the decision. A public exhibition of the designs took place in a vacant Belmont Street shop, starting in September 2011. A paper ballot was held at the exhibition for

'The Granite Web'.

the public to indicate their favoured design. The possibility of allowing the public to also vote on keeping Union Terrace Gardens in the ballot was rejected. The Friends of Union Terrace Gardens organised a picket for the duration. Many visitors to the exhibition told us that they had spoiled their ballot papers. It was later revealed that the design receiving the most votes from the public had not been the one that was finally selected by the jury, which chose a design called 'The Granite Web'.

The City Garden supporters could not escape the controversy over the plans: from their perspective, the furore was likely to blight the project for years. The politicians now proposed a public referendum on the issue.

The Friends of Union Terrace Gardens agreed to take part in the referendum at our annual general meeting. Following the design selection, we felt that the City Garden Project had gained new momentum and the juggernaut was on the move again. It was difficult to see what would stop it short of an expensive and chancy legal challenge. A referendum gave the chance to achieve a decisive knock-out blow to the City Garden Project, and our condition was that the referendum should be fair.

During the referendum campaign, the City Garden Project supporters argued that Aberdeen city centre needed to be transformed in order to regenerate its economy. The City Garden Project was described as vibrant and modern in contrast to the 'sunken hollow' of Union Terrace Gardens that never saw any sunlight. A brighter, better city centre was said to anchor the oil industry here longer by attracting professionals to Aberdeen who would otherwise have moved to Houston, Kuala Lumpur or Dubai. The Chamber of Commerce argued that the City Garden would turn Aberdeen into a tourist Mecca, and thus ensure a continuing local economy following the demise of North Sea oil. A vote for the City Garden Project was a vote for change, they said.

Our arguments were that Union Terrace Gardens are a vital part of Aberdeen's heritage, could be sympathetically enhanced, and that to replace them with a modern garden and structure would create a feature monstrously out of place in amongst the Victorian granite buildings of the city centre. We also argued that the economic risks were too great for the Council. Recent budget cuts had shown that the Council fiscal regime was

# UNION TERRACE GARDENS

At the BBC radio debate on Union Terrace Gardens at Queen's Cross Church Aberdeen on 16 February 2012. From the left: Callum McCaig (Leader of Aberdeen City Council Administration), Sir Ian Wood, Steven Duff (BBC), Lewis MacDonald MSP and Mike Shepherd (Chairman of the Friends of Union Terrace Gardens).

The referendum. Crawford Langley announces the results.

*The Friends of Union Terrace Gardens at the referendum count. From the left: Andrew MacGregor, Richard Pelling, Mike Shepherd (past President) and Robin McIntosh (President).*

under great strain. Aberdeen Council could not afford the risk of multi-million-pound borrowing for the project.

The referendum result was announced on 31 March 2012. There were 45,301 votes in favour of the City Garden Project and 41,145 against. In percentage terms, 52 per cent for and 48 per cent against. We narrowly lost. There was a bitter feeling about this as we thought the conduct of some of the various pro-City Garden Project supporters to have been grossly unfair. Whereas the campaigning groups were restricted to a maximum expenditure of £8,000, there had been nothing in the rules to prevent non-registered groups from launching an expensive and massive advertising blitz. One group described as The Vote for the City Garden Campaign paid for 238 radio adverts over a two-week period. These adverts (and twenty-six radio adverts that I paid for) were later deemed breaches of the broadcasting code, as they were considered political by nature. The night of the referendum result was our lowest moment. A number of us, including committee members Robin McIntosh, Richard Pelling and Andrew MacGregor, met in the Gardens under the crest, before heading off to the Prince of Wales pub for refreshments – emotional rescue for a sad day.

If the referendum had been intended as a palliative to calm unrest in the city over the Union Terrace Gardens affair, it hadn't worked. There was much discontent at what many thought was a stolen referendum. The massive imbalance in advertising spend had skewed the vote in the opinion of many. One campaigner compared the result to a football match, where one side had fielded twenty extra players after the match had started, and still only won 1–0.

Council elections would be held two months later on 3 May 2012. The SNP had been privately hoping to see a majority of councillors elected, so that they could form an administration without any need to seek coalition partners. The political pundits thought this unlikely, but still predicted the SNP to end up as the largest group in the council.

The SNP had been linked to the City Garden Project, and were hoping for its success. The Labour party opposed the City Garden project and pledged to scrap it if they got the chance. The other main party, the Liberal Democrats, were split on the issue with three councillors, Martin Greig, Jennifer Stewart and Ian Yuill, having opposed the scheme. One of our committee members, Kenny Watt, had provided a website giving information concerning where the candidates standing for election stood with respect to the Union Terrace Gardens issue. He had tried contacting as many of the candidates as possible. Some whom I suspected to be pro-City Garden Project were non-committal when asked. In spite of the referendum result, candidate endorsement for the City Garden Project had been somewhat subdued in the lead up to the election. Kenny's website was widely distributed and had been intended as a voting guide only.

The Council vote was a surprise to many, not least the Labour party. They found themselves with the largest number of new councillors at seventeen – ahead of the SNP. This was not quite enough to form a majority, though (which is twenty-two in a council with forty-three members). They did manage to secure the agreement of the Conservatives and Independents to form a coalition led by Barney Crockett. There is no doubt that several controversial local issues in recent years had played a part, including a proposed third Don crossing in Tillydrone and a new football stadium in Cove and Kincorth. However, I believe the Union Terrace Gardens controversy had a significant influence. The number of Labour party councillors increased substantially and all three Liberal Democrats who had supported the preservation of Union Terrace Gardens were returned in spite of their party's poor showing elsewhere. The Friends group received numerous comments from people who admit to having changed their normal voting pattern because they were so upset at what they saw as a cynical campaign strategy by the City Garden supporters in the referendum. It looks as if the referendum result had an unexpected sting in its tail.

The new council were now called upon to vote on the business case for the City Gardens Project, specifically to approve the Council borrowing of £70 million for the project through a TIF scheme. The report for the business case had been prepared by Council officers. There were many problems with the report; indeed the prominent Scottish economist Tony Mackay, who had been commissioned by the council Labour group to analyse the report, went on to describe it as misleading and criticised it for making extravagant and unexplained claims.

I was shocked when I read the report. The private sector funding for the City Garden Project was still £15 million short, and as such the Council did not have enough money to cover the £140 million nominal cost of the project. A further problem was that there were no detailed final costs. The £140 million quoted cost of the project had not changed since the original feasibility study compiled three and a half years earlier. This meant that the councillors were being asked to commit to a multi-million-pound project without knowing what the final bill would be. This was crazy.

The author of the report was required to demonstrate that the TIF project would create extra business that would not have existed otherwise. This was not easy to prove, as business in Aberdeen is buoyant because of the oil industry. The methodology used was to send a questionnaire to local developers and property companies asking them if the City Garden Project were to proceed would this specifically encourage them to fund new projects in Aberdeen. Not one replied. Council officials then phoned around and this time they got seven replies. The responders told the Council officials that any construction plans they had for Aberdeen would go ahead anyway, with or without the proposed plans for the city centre. This was not helpful.

So the Council staff had to find another way to justify the business case for TIF funding. They then produced a discussion document containing their key assumptions under-pinning the economics of the TIF scheme and giving the economic projections based on these assumptions. This was sent to the developers for comment. There were no replies. How then could the council staff justify the business case for borrowing £70 million? According to the business report: 'No recipients provided any further views, implicitly suggesting acceptance of the projections.'

This was the crux of the business case for the City Garden Project. Having accepted this highly dubious 'justification' based on the silent yet seemingly approving business community, the report then stated that the project would: 'generate up to 6,560 full-time equivalent jobs and an average of £115.1 million per annum of economic growth over twenty-five years.'

The business case for the City Garden Project was a pack of cards waiting to totter. The Council voted on 22 August 2012 and rejected it by two votes. Without public funding, the City Garden Project was dead. The next day Sir Ian Wood told the chief executive of Aberdeen Council that he was withdrawing his offer of £50 million. The offer actually lingered on the table for over a year, but there was no enthusiasm within the new Council to do anything about it. Union Terrace Gardens had yet again survived to be enjoyed by future generations of Aberdonians.

Chapter Fourteen

# SOME RANDOM THOUGHTS

The City Square Project (CSP) set out 'to create an accessible space that will integrate the Union Street retail and business thoroughfare with the cultural heart of His Majesty's Theatre and the existing Art Gallery whilst providing the context for a new Contemporary Arts Centre.' Aberdeen city centre is small however, and culture and shops sit in close proximity. From the Music Hall, along Union Terrace to the Central Library, H M Theatre and the Art Gallery, then down Schoolhill to a couple of malls and Marks & Spencer, all bounded by Union Street to the south – all are already reasonably integrated through existing 'accessible space'. It was felt by some that if Union Terrace Gardens were to be decked to pavement level to allow for an Arts Centre, that would be surely be the Trojan Horse for future commercial development and the complete loss of Union Bridge.

In those early days I attended a burgess meeting in the Douglas Hotel where the platform party consisted of Sir Ian Wood and two others. 'You'll know by my accent I'm not from Aberdeen,' said the principal speaker – a good beginning, of course! He announced that the City Square Project would have water features and statues, perhaps unaware that the Denburn had been flowing through the area since time immemorial. It would not be beyond the miracles of modern engineering science to reinstate the burn outwith its culvert and create something integral and attractive – a waterfall perhaps? – without introducing an extraneous water source. As for statues, the Gardens are flanked by some of the finest statues in Europe. There was mention too – and this was a point made verbally and in press releases from the CSP people and their architects – that the project would reunite communities, apparently parted by Union Terrace Gardens. This was not so. Sociable evenings in the future Gardens brought people from around the area together. The communities were broken up, Mutton Brae by the arrival of the Denburn Valley Junction Railway in 1865–1867 and Schoolhill, Blackfriars and Woolmanhill by the building of Rosemount Viaduct in 1886–1868. They were poor areas and their loss was seen as inevitable.

Sir Ian Wood stated at that briefing that the City Square Project at ground level would not be a commercial development. But vague rumours were circulating of underground car parks being used in conjunction with the Triple Kirks development and with the possible demolition and redevelopment of the Denburn car park and adjoining site. The author John Aberdein wrote to Aberdeen City Council in those early days, highlighting the lack of information about the project:

> The reason that so many people are entirely wary of the City Square Project as it now stands, is that it is a very unusual beast: a chameleon with three wooden legs. Is there to be a double-storey car park? We hear changing stories about that. Why? Is there to be a retail presence? No. Yes. If yes, why? How would that help an already retail-denuded Union Street? Is there to be an underground art gallery, an entombed conference centre? Point: we already have an Art Gallery and a Conference Centre, above ground, in the light.

The thought of losing Union Terrace Gardens was saddening. I couldn't imagine them not being there. A remnant of the levels of the pre-Union Street town, they punch above their weight in a city centre that is so small. To have a real valley there, resembling the policies of some great house, was an amazing bonus, and I disliked the continuing derogation of the Gardens as some dark and gloomy hole or awkward sort of corner impeding one's movement from one shopping mall to the next.

I remember standing at the old C&A building on the Bridge Street corner and looking across to the Gardens, to where the railway and road ran below, and to Belmont Street. The area in question was vast. A number of questions sprang to mind. How would the Gardens marry with Belmont Street? How could they think of destroying the Belmont Street skyline? How long would it take to remove thousands of tons of the present Gardens,

*Award-winning author John Aberdein with the Gardens behind him.*

the great granite staircases, rock, soil, trees, given the poor access? How many years would the city centre be in turmoil? It had enough problems as it was.

The railway and dual carriageway would be part of the scheme, covered in so that further CSP structures could be erected on top. Rail passengers would lose views of the Gardens, the best entrance to the city. The most appropriate comparison was with the Union Square complex on Guild Street, completed in 2009, a straightforward construction on flat, empty land – the former goods yard of the old Caledonian Railway in fact – with good access. That cost £250 million.

During my travels over the following year or two I had time to size up the twin inspirations of Sir Ian Wood's vision, a combination of the Italian piazza and New York's Central Park. These did not seem appropriate

*Union Terrace Gardens writ large. The colourful Sunken Gardens at the Butchart Gardens on Vancouver Island.*

replacements for Union Terrace Gardens. A more suitable exemplar was the stunningly beautiful Butchart Gardens in Victoria on Vancouver Island, which reminds one of the Aberdeen Gardens, though on a much bigger scale. They began to take form in 1909 when Jennie Butchart transformed a disused quarry, whose limestone had been used to supply her husband's Portland cement factory, into a delightful Sunken Garden. In 2004 they were recognised as a National Historic Site of Canada.

The press meanwhile had anticipated a struggle for Union Terrace Gardens between the plucky Davids of Peacock Visual Arts and the Goliaths of the Wood camp, which was encircled by a panoply of advisers, consultants, agencies, stakeholder groups, key players and public relations people. But a clear-cut battle of struggling artists versus the oil billionaire and his cohorts it was not to be, for there were three groups in the conflict at this time. Many Aberdonians wanted, first and foremost, the restoration of Union Street and the return of some top-quality shops there. As far as

# SOME RANDOM THOUGHTS

Union Terrace Gardens was concerned, the only change required, apart from an increased budget to allow more planting and upgrading, was the refurbishment and reopening of the Victorian toilets, and the removal of any undesirable characters who still hung around there.

The findings of a feasibility study by Halliday Fraser Munro (HFM) into raising Union Terrace Gardens, commissioned by Scottish Enterprise, were published in June 2009, containing useful information. But the Gardens as an Enemy of the People, a central theme in the conflict, was again to the fore.

'It is the (Denburn) valley itself which creates the physical barrier right in the heart of the city causing so many of the area's difficulties.' Someone had missed the fact that the problem has already been taken care of. Union Bridge and Rosemount Viaduct were built to surmount the barrier of the Denburn Valley.

'The gardens are difficult to access and overshadowed for most of the year.' . . . 'Access to the gardens is to all intents limited to the fit and able.'

*'A dark hole in the ground that acts as a barrier . . .' Well, perhaps not. The city crest, centre, has been a much-admired, integral part of the Gardens since the early days.*

In fact if you can walk down steps, albeit with the assistance of a handrail and a walking stick, you have three centrally sited entrances to choose from. Entrance for buggies, wheelchairs and the handicapped in general is at the north end by the Lower Denburn, the little road which starts opposite the Denburn car park at the foot of Skene Street, and which runs down the side of His Majesty's Theatre and under the Denburn Viaduct. That was the way the sheep used to enter the Denburn Meadows long ago. This entrance deserves to be better signposted, and that is in hand as I write.

A similar negative philosophy prevailed on the ACSEF website of those days. It described the Gardens as: 'A dark hole in the ground that acts as a barrier to the movement of people around the city.' . . . 'The Gardens . . . do not contribute to the connectivity within the city centre and the difficulty in accessing them means that they cannot perform the role of a gathering and meeting place which a real heart of the city should have.' I have lived in Aberdeen all my life and have never felt the Gardens to be a dark hole or an obstacle to getting around. I used to enjoy walking along the promenade beside the Garden's arches instead of the Union Terrace pavement, and

*A magnificent view of the Arches. They were formed when Union Terrace had to expand out over the Gardens.*

have started to do so again. There seemed no appreciation that the Gardens were a unique symbol of our heritage, marking the place where the new city took over from the medieval town.

One of the bright spots of this depressing campaign, was the appearance of an odd bag of City Square Project supporters – or Garden Project as it became – who took up their stance outside the north end of the Gardens and were featured prominently in the local press. Kicking off in February 2010 was Sir Alex Ferguson, followed by other enthusiasts whose connections with the Gardens, like those of the Legend himself, seemed tenuous. I recall a nightclub manager, a PR man, another football manager, an oilman, an ice cream manufacturer, the 'here today gone tomorrow' man from Creative Scotland and hotel and restaurant people. Guessing who might come along next was an enjoyable pastime and predicting possible personalities became more and more outrageous. A favourite mantra of these CSP supporters was to describe the Gardens as 'underused' and 'underutilised'. Dr Adrian G Marshall wrote to the press:

> It has been argued in support of the proposal that Aberdeen's Union Terrace Gardens are little used. It is a fundamental misconception that for landscapes to be of value they must be entered; surely it is untrue that only those who climb Lochnagar value it? Thus, although I have not entered the Gardens for months, I have appreciated their presence countless times over the weeks as I have walked past, something I am sure is true for many citizens.

Dr Caroline Paterson too, wrote an excellent letter:

> Among all that has been said and written for and against the various plans for the future of Union Terrace Gardens, I have seen nothing which truly expresses the unique value of the Denburn Valley as an open space in the centre of our city. That the gardens themselves are 'under-used' is not the point. The open views across the valley from Union Bridge, Union Terrace or Rosemount Viaduct offer calm and relief from the bustle of the city streets around.

ACSEF organised a public consultation based on the HFM feasibility study which ran from 11 January until 5 March 2010 with interviews carried out by Weber Shandwick, 'one of the world's leading global public relations firms.' I imagined an art gallery foyer bedecked with artists' impressions and models of possible designs, but discovered the venues were of a more modest nature. I found my nearest stand to be small, tucked at the rear of the Trinity Centre and manned by a young woman from Edinburgh. She told me the consultation was being funded by Scottish Enterprise, that she didn't know much about Aberdeen, but advised that the balustrades and statues in Union Street (sic) would be kept. I was given a postcard which asked: 'Do you Support the City Square Project?' As with those attempting to answer the same question online, there was a bias towards a 'Yes' vote, which surely militated against the 'transparency of the process' referred to in the Scottish Enterprise Project Brief. The postcard which could be detached and sent off allowed inadequate space for objection. It was at the back of a booklet produced by the City Square Project and featured the usual artwork of a computerised, uninspired public space with mostly young people walking about aimlessly: 'A thriving cosmopolitan café culture is represented by about ten tables, surrounded by uncomfortable looking chairs. It is not surprising that all are empty. In one picture the view of the magnificent Rosemount Viaduct panorama has been reduced to a few lumpish, disembodied turrets. Another shows a man wheeling a suitcase along what looks like a deserted airport corridor while the accompanying caption reads: 'A Place for everyone to enjoy the city centre.' Annie Lennox, the Aberdeen-born pop star, is photographed in full voice, giving the impression that she would be performing in the Square. In fact she has been a whole-hearted opponent of the scheme since it was first announced and made public her objections in no uncertain manner. The booklet was later withdrawn.

As part of the consultation, various focus groups – schoolchildren, arts people, councillors, and a number of other organisations – were asked by Weber Shandwick for their opinions. We had heard many proclamations about the global importance of the project, so the comments of those organisations opposed to it made a refreshing change. Aberdeen Civic

## SOME RANDOM THOUGHTS

Forum expressed doubts about the funding, traffic management, the decking over of the Gardens, the lack of detail in the proposals, and did not approve of the plan as it stood. Ashley and Broomhill Community Council felt that if there were a proven need or demand for a Square it could be created when St Nicolas House was demolished. Ruthrieston Residents' Association felt it was the wrong project for the times, in the wrong site, outdated and ill-considered. All except one member ('and he was swithering') of the Queen's Cross and Harlaw Community Council spoke firmly against the proposals. All five points made were sensible, and the last one a corker:

1. We do not wish to see the destruction of the Gardens. 2. The proposals are ill-conceived and would create further problems than they would resolve. 3. The business case presented is tenuous and unproven. 4. Public money is in scant supply and there are more immediate and worthy needs. 5. If the proposers feel strongly about leaving a future legacy for the citizens of Aberdeen then they should dig deeper into their minds for a more suitable project and finance its role in the development of the layout of the city.

When sending their subscriptions to join the Friends of Union Terrace Gardens the fondness of Aberdonians, old and young, for the Gardens was palpable.

Patricia Davidson: 'I am appalled at the changes which are being considered in relation to Union Terrace Gardens. They are unique to Aberdeen. The site is more attractive than Edinburgh's Princes Street Gardens and no-one is trying to change that.' Mrs I Reid: 'We have spent the afternoon in the Gardens enjoying the entertainment for Tartan Day. At street level the entertainment wouldn't be the same at all.' Margaret A M Greig: 'Large numbers of mature trees, some of them more than 100 years old, will have to be cut down. The greenery shown in the plans will not be mature for generations.' Brian Cowie: 'My heart will be broken if the bulldozers are allowed in.' Joan Robertson: 'I was born in Aberdeen and have lived all my life in the area. I feel very strongly that Union Terrace Gardens should not be "filled in" to create an area which would not be unique.'

# UNION TERRACE GARDENS

*The Trees of Union Terrace Gardens.*

Margaret I D Colburn: 'Our Gardens are special and just need improving and made safe. I'm a senior citizen and value this unique facility.' Katrine Graham-Yooll: 'The Gardens should be preserved and not modernised.' Tillydrone Community Council OAPs: 'The Gardens were here long before Sir Ian Wood and his friends, so they should be here for us and our children to enjoy for the future.'

Historic Scotland raised excellent points: 'The Gardens and their surroundings are key elements of this part of Aberdeen and the wider historic environment of which they form part. They contribute hugely to the high quality of the local townscape and as well as providing a green space. The Gardens and their bridges, buildings and balustrade terraces are central to the character and understanding of the conservation area.'

Throughout the campaign I was puzzled by slogans such as 'together we can do it' which were at odds with the apparent determination to employ foreign experts, architects and gardening designers. (Scottish architects were sceptical, pointing out that the project lacked the funds for completion.) There was another dichotomy, between the dearth of hard facts and practical information on one hand and the flowery PR statements on the fantastic nature and global importance of the project on the on the other. 'It will create a buzz,' said Malcolm Reading, head of a London firm of architectural consultants employed to run the design competition, 'a sense of something happening, interest from around the world, global media attention, local dialogue, an enriched environment for everyone.'

A 'jury' was empanelled, chaired by ex-Aberdeen University principal Sir Duncan Rice, and including an 'urban regeneration guru'. Six designs were chosen, prompting the inevitable criticism – why should a bunch of unelected people decide how the centre of Aberdeen should look? It is perhaps worth emphasising that, as a result of a Freedom of Information inquiry, of the two competing designs at the final stage of the competition, the one which replicated some of the features of the current Gardens won the top number of votes cast at the exhibition: 5,746. The ultimate winner 'The Granite Web' design had only 1,378 votes. What then was the point of the competition?

The name was not particularly apt. There was no 'Web', only thick flyovers reminiscent of the 1930s Busby Berkeley movie sets where chorus girls used to come tap-dancing down. And there was no indication that the 'Web' would be made of granite. The assumption was that it would be made of concrete. The use of the word 'granite' seemed to be a sop to Aberdeen and some pathways were to have granite chuckies. Others would use shreddings from felled trees.

However I did find the architects Diller Scofidio & Renfro's exposition of their award winning design a great *tour de force*. It deserves an award of its own:

> The Aberdeen City Garden will fuse Nature and Culture into a vital social network at the heart of the city. Rejecting the classical model of the cultural building isolated on the green, the Garden extends the surrounding urban fabric as an elastic web of three-dimensional

interconnections across its site. The warp and weft of the urban lines support both park and cultural activities within a resilient fabric of layered programs, conjoining history with the contemporary and the urbane with the pastoral. Stretching across the historic river site, this parkland web is permeable, revealing a multi-tiered archaeology while connecting to the city's emergent future.

And a favourite piece of artwork, much used in 'Granite Web' promotions, included a brilliant sunset over H M Theatre – which lies to the north.

At last, to the relief of many, and as recorded in the previous chapter, the saga came to a halt when Aberdeen City Council voted to reject the City Garden Project on 22 August 2012.

Chapter Fifteen

# IN RETROSPECT

In the battle to save Union Terrace Gardens, Katie Guthrie and the film-maker Fraser Denholm set the ball rolling with their 'I Heart UTG' campaign for Peacock Visual Arts. Steve Bothwell of Café 52 writes, 'They should be credited with getting the passion in the citizens of this city going for saving the Gardens.' No one has worked harder than Steve himself. One of the livewires of this affair, he formed his own action group, Common Good, Aberdeen. He has spent his own cash, livened things up and tried on two occasions to establish a café in the Gardens, and to introduce children's swings.

I was impressed that Jimmy Milne – Dr James S Milne CBE DBA, Chairman and Managing Director of the Balmoral Group, and one of North-east Scotland's most successful entrepreneurs – nailed his colours firmly to the mast and gave outstanding support to the Friends and their aims during the campaign.

I admired the way Councillor Martin Greig of the Liberal Democrats consistently voted against the City Garden Project. He had expressed concern about the largely underground two and a half acres within a proposed new cultural building – a lot of empty internal space in search of a purpose. 'I am sure a proposal to develop Union Terrace Gardens will be back in a form of eternal recurrence,' he says. Sadly, he is probably right.

I thought the Helena Torry episode was a good prank. A tailor's dummy, Helena was dressed up as an Aberdeen housewife and entered as a candidate in Sir Ian Wood's ward for the coming council election, to express her opposition to the City Garden Project. She was eventually unmasked, but all credit to Helena's owner, Renée Slater of Torry, for imagination and a bit of brass neck. There was a later court case but fortunately that came to nothing.

*Unsung heroes. The Union Terrace gardeners have kept the Gardens immaculate, through thick and thin. Ian Griffiths, Gardener, right, with Environmental Operative Jim Tough.*

I enjoyed the Mackay Intervention, in which the leading economist Tony Mackay grew ever more appalled as he read the business case of the City Garden Project produced by Aberdeen City Garden Trust as means of acquiring TIF funding. 'The estimates are ludicrous,' he cried, and finally advised Aberdeen City Council to put it in the waste bin.

Moving on to the referendum, I was unhappy about the fact that unregistered parties were not constrained by the rules and were able to spend very large sums on advertising in favour of the CGP. That should have led to the cancellation of the referendum until some firm, fair rules were put in place.

What could one do to express doubts, worries and downright opposition? In spite of the fact that the local press favoured the CGP, their Readers' Letters gave both sides and there was a 'Readers' Comments' facility on the Aberdeen Journals website for a time where a lively discussion followed relevant articles. Its content was heterogeneous: long, intelligent, serious pieces that were virtual articles; short witty comments; arguments between readers on both sides. The subject was debated and discussed on BBC and STV though I did regret the demise of Grampian Television. Former producer Alan Cowie told me that he would have loved staging one of the station's big debates on the issue.

The Friends of Union Terrace Gardens are on Facebook, there are articles in the online weekly *Aberdeen Voice* (editor Fred Wilkinson) by John Aberdein and Mike Shepherd who has also written a number of pieces for the national press including the *Guardian* and its Blog. There is the brilliant investigative journalism of Suzanne Kelly. Her articles on what was wrong about the referendum are worth tracking down in the *Aberdeen Voice*. Former head teacher Douglas Marr has written about the Gardens in *Scottish Review*. In the issue of 8 July 2010 he did not mince his words:

> The project's supporters, and above all, the business community, have expressed their contempt for the city, its people and its heritage, The combination of a handful of strong-minded millionaires and weak-willed councillors has prevailed. Their breath-taking arrogance that they know best is coming within a hair's breadth of depriving Aberdeen of a feature (Union Terrace Gardens) that most other cities would die for.

There was the occasional witty and succinct coverage in *Private Eye* by 'Piloti', the distinguished architectural historian, Gavin Stamp, in his *Nooks and Corners*. Alex Mitchell, editor of the Aberdeen Civic Society *Newsletter*, is a droll critic of the project. As he wrote in the early days: 'Wir puir toon is hurtling like *RMS Titanic* towards a metaphorical iceberg of debt and all these guys can think of to do is to rearrange the deckchairs!' In the dark, early days I was cheered by an article in the *Sunday Herald* by Joanna Blythman, 'The Granite City is in thrall to the Philistines'. The Gardens also have a section in Owen Hatherley's *A New Kind of Bleak*. Andrew MacGregor has collected a superb archive of the affair which will have considerable historic value.

This affair has produced its own vocabulary. In no particular order: connectivity, iconic, revamp, unlock, transitional, walkability, vibrant, aspirational, global, cultural, underused, underutilised, transformational, business leaders, business bosses, business chiefs, top officials, key stakeholders, global energy hub, footfall, footprint, world class, urban realm, the wow factor, tipping point, spearheading, key players, synergies, revenue stream, overarching, portal.

I liked the blogs. Lenathehyena was always worth reading and Auchterness is hilarious, an unbelievable toady. I will leave you to guess who his three great heroes are. In his blog, Bertie the wire-haired terrier wrote a good résumé of a visit to the Gardens at the height of the affair. 'So many splendid trees to sniff, places to run about, and no boring "dogs mustn't do this and that" signs.' I was alarmed by the inability of those outwith Aberdeen, and some within, to realise that the £50 million was not a gift, but a contribution, and a serious debt problem was a reality. Sir Ian has made it clear that no other project was of interest to him. Like many others I found his conviction that the City Garden Project would guarantee the continuing prosperity of the city hard to accept. If he had decided on a project that would have been undoubtedly popular – if not global – the restoration of the Victorian toilets in Union Terrace Gardens or the refurbishment and reopening of the Bon-Accord Baths, much less costly even when suitably endowed against depreciation, how different things would have been.

Most of all, I admired a most impressive speech from Denis Yule on behalf of the Friends, in relation to the TIF business case which he gave to Aberdeen City Council in August 2012:

> The City Garden Project has been allowed to dominate the Council's thinking and has formed a distraction from the really important issues for the future of Aberdeen. It has been promoted vigorously by a small group of private businessmen using all the public relations pressure, pleading and persuasion that money can buy. The way that TIF is supposed to work is that the Council should decide on its priorities then persuade the private sector to invest, not the other way round as has happened here. The Council should be leading, not following the private sector.

The Friends of Union Terrace Gardens worked hard throughout, leafleting in town in all weathers, lobbying the Council, writing on the internet. They

IN RETROSPECT

*Bertie the blogging wire-haired terrier surveys the Gardens as he thinks out his piece. Below him is the 'Friendship Tree', a Himalayan Pine.*

held their first picnic in the Gardens on 12 June 2010. It had been assumed by the local press that this would be a protest meeting, but it wasn't. It was a very friendly gathering enjoyed by people of all ages. Old friends met up again, new contacts were made, councillors who had opposed the CGP introduced themselves. Everyone was discussing ideas for the future of the Gardens. This was the start of many gatherings in this dark, 'unused and inaccessible place', ceilidhs, and in June 2012 Queen's Jubilee Tea Party with music, hosted by the Steve Bothwell and his mother, Dorothy, who has been a power house in this whole affair. The colourful celebration of Eid at the end of Ramadan, the Muslim month of fasting, has become an annual event, as has the Masked Ball of the Anchor Charity.

The task of the Friends has moved from campaigning to nurturing and improving, publicising, working in the Gardens as volunteers hand in hand with environmental staff of Aberdeen City Council. In February 2013 they suggested the installation of nesting boxes as part of National Nestbox Week

*The amazing Queen's Jubilee tea party at Union Terrace Gardens. Mrs Dorothy Bothwell did all the baking.*

to encourage more birds into the area. The Council's Countryside Rangers provided the building materials and Aberdeen City Council's Tree Squad helped with the installation. The Friends raised £650 for a rhododendron walk near the Gents' toilets, their contribution matched by the City Council. With members of the Volunteering Students Association they painted the Arches where necessary one Saturday, applying 140 litres of paint.

They have reintroduced the famous draughts. There are plans to create a wild meadow studded with poppies in the field below the city's War Memorial. They were involved in the celebration for the arrival of the Queen's Baton Relay in Aberdeen, prior to the 2014 Commonwealth Games. They have manned craft tables, raised money for picnic benches and scrubbed down and painted what appears to be miles of railings. They

*The festival of Eid in the Gardens, marking the end of the month-long Muslim fast of Ramadan. Lord Provost George Adam with some of the children and their parents.*

are involved in the City's Winter Festival, and much more and now receive modest funding from the Common Good Fund. In spring 2015, they were planning to plant one million crocuses.

In January 2014 Aberdeen was selected from more than 1,000 entrants to compete in the Royal Horticultural Society's 50th Britain in Bloom UK finals and Union Terrace Gardens was one of the sites visited. I went round part of the way with the judges and we looked at the magnificent city crest, bedded in annually but like the handsome urns, dating back to the early days. Three small flower-beds laid out above the crest commemorated the 100th anniversary of the outbreak of the Great War. We also looked at the

*The War Memorial rises above the Gardens.*

*A group of Friends volunteers. Chairman Robin McIntosh is third right.*

*New graduates in the Gardens. The Robert Gordon University holds its graduation ceremonies just across Rosemount Viaduct at H M Theatre.*

*A fine elm in the old Corbie Heugh.*

fine arcade of arches and the remarkable vistas all round, uniquely viewed from the Gardens. That October Aberdeen was awarded Gold at the Britain in Bloom awards.

To end on another happy note, it's good to report that the wooded banks of the old Corbie Heugh are still there and contain fine specimens, some over 200 years old, including Scotch elms, survivors of the plantings of 1770s. They are among the last remnants of mature elm trees in Northern Europe. They are free of Dutch Elm Disease, for though the Dutch Elm Beetle has been seen in the Gardens it does not attack Scotch Elms which it does not like.

# SELECT BIBLIOGRAPHY

There are no books devoted entirely to Union Terrace Gardens but a good place to start is Andy Wightman's Report, *Union Terrace Gardens Historic and Legal Status* (2011), which can be downloaded from the internet. It is full of salient points and good leads.

The biographies of Archibald Simpson, 2006, and Tudor Johnny – John Smith, 2007, by David Miller (both Librario) are invaluable tools for any student of the architecture of nineteeth-century Aberdeen.

Extracts from the *Burgh of Aberdeen Council Register,* 12 & 13 September 1745, ed John Stuart, give an account of General Sir George Cope's cantonment with over 2,000 redcoats in the Doocot Brae in 1745. That action likely triggered off municipal involvement in the control of the future Gardens. Scottish Burgh Records Society, Spalding (1848).

Francis Douglas, *A General Description of the East Coast of Scotland,* (Paisley 1782), provides an account of the future Union Terrace Gardens as a pleasure park.

Rev. George Skene Keith's unsurpassed *General View of the Agriculture of Aberdeenshire* (1811), gives us the 'Denburn Meadows' and the presence of sheep.

The *Annals of Woodside and Newhills*, Patrick Morgan, (David Wylie and Son Aberdeen, 1886), makes reference to a sale by Marischal College of a feu on the west side of Belmont Street at the junction with Schoolhill in 1785. The purchasers were Gordon, Barron & Co, owners of the cotton mill, Woodside Works. This provides a clue to the role of the future Gardens as the Great Bleachery.

Aberdeen City Library has compiled a package of *Aberdeen Journal* reports from January 1865 to April 1879 which give a lively verbatim account of council meetings and decisions, developments and procrastinations which led to the eventual creation of the Gardens.

William Robbie's *Aberdeen: Its Traditions and History* (1893), discusses contemporary attitudes towards the creation of the Gardens, and in particular, the cost of the balustrading, and pronounces it all worthwhile.

William Carnie *Reporting Reminiscences Vol. 2*, (Aberdeen University Press, 1903), reports on James Matthews' plan: 'here then was the seed sown for the harvest of labour which was to bring around the wondrous change'.

*Aberdeen in Bygone* Days by Robert Anderson, (*Aberdeen Daily Journal Office*, 1910), is full of information about the early days of the Denburn area, but watch your eyes.

Just outwith the Gardens though still in the Denburn Valley, an account of the early ups and downs of the Triple Kirks is provided by Alexander Gammie in *The Churches of Aberdeen* (1909).

W Dobson Chapman & Charles F Riley's *Granite City*, (Batsford, London, 1952) have little to say in their lifeless prose about the Gardens but complain about the dirt and smell caused by the railway. This is no longer a problem, but it seems that it was the steam trains with their attendant soot and steam that first gave rise to demands that the line be enclosed.

Back numbers and annuals of the old *Bon Accord* weekly provide photographs of the amphitheatre kitted out as a stage, and the various activities there, including fun and games for the children and Highland dancing.

# SELECT BIOGRAPHY

In the April 1983 edition of *Leopard Magazine*, John Souter wrote about the development of Union Terrace.

W A Brogden's *Architecture of a City* (Ashgate 2011), provides a fascinating perspective of the Gardens. Plans by Robert Gordon's architectural students are featured and the author gives an appropriately tart comment on those seeking to raise the Gardens to street level 'without considering climate, topography, or the existence of numerous listed buildings.'

In his excellent *Robert Gordon University – A History*, (Aberdeen, 2002), Henry Ellington describes John Gray's benefactions, which created the Gardens' wider environment.

There are enough modern reports on Union Terrace Gardens and the Denburn Valley to cover over the rail track and the Denburn Dual Carriageway, but one of the more informative (though determined to discredit the Gardens) is the Halliday Fraser Munro Technical Feasibility Study of June 2011, funded by Scottish Enterprise. Aberdeen City Council's papers on Landscape Strategy (available on the internet) over the years is also interesting to read in view of developments. A report by Crawford Langley on the Referendum gives interesting information on how to hold a referendum.

The *Historical Newspaper Articles* series on Union Terrace Gardens, courtesy of Robin McIntosh, were invaluable both for local daily and national press coverage.

# INDEX

**A**

*Aberdeen Journal*, the ix, 54, 61, 139, 164–165, 220, 230
Aberdeen City Council 151,153, 171, 180, 182, 184, 187–188, 190–194, 196, 198, 201–206, 208, 218, 220, 222–224, 231
Aberdeen City Garden Trust (ACGT) 198, 200, 220
Aberdeen City and Shire Economic Future (ACSEF) 190–194, 198, 212, 214
Aberdeen Civic Forum 214–215
Aberdeen Civic Society 147, 154, 221
Aberdeen Railway Company 139
Aberdeen Savings Banks (ASB) 90–92, 108, 110, 146
Albyn Design Associates 177
Alex Hadden & Sons 7, 11
Anderson, Alexander 70–71, 76, 78–80, 100
Anderson, Robert 34, 46, 127, 162, 230

**B**

Back Wynd 5, 7, 31–32
Backs of Belmont 142, 155–157
Baron Carlo Marochetti 100–101
Beattie, James Forbes 48, 55–59, 61, 63, 158, 161
Belmont Street xi, xii, 5, 7, 10, 21, 29, 31–32, 34, 41, 44, 48, 51, 61, 63, 66, 82, 87, 129, 133–136, 138, 142–143, 146–147, 154–157, 177, 182, 200, 208, 229
Belmont Street United Free Church 136, 143
Betjeman, John xii, 146, 155
Bleachfields 21–22, 25, 26–28, 30, 37
Bon Accord Church 64, 76–77
Bon Accord Free Church 64, 74, 78, 92
Bonnie Prince Charlie *see Charles Edward Stuart*
Boulton, William 82–83, 85, 90
Bow Brig 2, 7, 9–14, 17, 27, 33, 38, 162, 165
Britain in Bloom Awards 175, 226, 228

Burns, Robert viii, 75, 108, 110, 117
Byron, Catherine 24–25

**C**
Carden Place 9, 123
Carnie, William 99, 230
Chinese bridges 29–30, 33, 37, 40, 47
Citymoves Dance Agency 149, 187
City Garden Project, the 187, 190–196, 198, 200–201, 203–208, 213–214, 218–220, 222
City Square Project, the see *City Garden Project*
Collie's Brig 1, 50
Condor Projects (Scotland) 179
Cope, John 15–17, 22
Corbie Heugh xi, xii, 1, 3, 10, 13–16, 22–25, 27, 30, 36, 38–44, 46–48, 50, 52, 54–55, 64–66, 77, 136, 185, 228
Corinthian Scheme, the 130–131

**D**
Denburn xi, 1–3, 5, 7, 9–12, 15, 20, 22, 25–29, 32–34, 39–41, 43–44, 49–50, 57, 83, 125, 131, 134, 139–140, 142, 157, 182, 207, 212
Denburn Bleachfield *see Bleachfields*
Denburn Dual Carriageway 84–85, 157, 160, 180
Denburn Meadows 7, 9, 54, 212

Denburn Road 83, 89, 142, 155, 157–158, 177, 180, 182
Denburn Terrace 41–44, 51–52, 63, 85, 125
Denburn Valley xi, xii, 1–6, 9–10, 13, 15, 19, 37, 39, 43, 48–49, 57, 71, 81–83, 90, 102, 123, 125, 130–131, 134, 139, 142, 158, 198, 211, 213
Denburn Valley Junction Railway 40, 47, 53, 85, 125, 139–142, 158, 208
Denburn Viaduct viii, 83–85, 89–90, 109, 157, 161, 182, 212
Diamond Place 77, 90, 92, 110
Disruption, the 78, 131–132, 134–135, 139, 143
Doocot Brae 13, 15, 19, 30, 229
Doocot Croft 2, 13–14, 16, 22, 65
Douglas, Francis 11, 26, 28–30, 33, 229
Duff, Alexander 23–24
Duff, James 22–25
Duke of Cumberland 17, 129
Dutch Elm Disease viii, 228

**E**
East Free Church 63, 122, 132–133, 143–144, 147
Esson Properties 149, 151

**F**
Feus 21, 26–28, 40, 42–43, 48, 50, 57, 60, 65, 77, 83, 85, 229

Forty-Five, the 16, 22
Four Neukit Garden 3–4, 10, 43, 47
Fraser, GM 125, 134
Freedom of Information Act 191, 217
Friends of Union Terrace Gardens xii, 187, 194–195, 201–203, 205, 215, 219, 221–224, 227

## G
Gaelic Lane 7, 30–32, 34, 133
George Gordon *see Lord Byron*
Gilcomston Free Kirk 142
Gordon, James xii, 1–3, 5, 13
Gordon, Robert 1–2, 18–19, 34–36, 46, 84, 117, 119–120, 177, 227, 231
Gordon of Khartoum 117
Grammar School 34–36, 41, 43, 51, 53, 80, 118, 120, 122
Grampian Enterprise Ltd 149, 180–182
Grand Hotel *see Palace Hotel*
Granite Web, the 200–201, 217–218
Gray, John xii, 71, 87, 108, 119, 121, 123, 143, 231
Gray's School of Art 35, 71–72, 108, 118–122
Grazing 9, 20, 22, 26, 30, 37, 47
Great Bleachery, the xii, 33, 35, 37–38, 40, 229

Great North of Scotland Railway (GNSR) 52–53, 59, 74–76, 83, 139, 142–143
Guestrow, the 17, 19, 171–172

## H
Hadden, Baillie 11, 38
Halliday Fraser Munro 151, 160, 211, 231
High Free Church 143–144
His Majesty's Theatre 9, 84, 87, 89, 95–96, 103, 162, 174–175, 187, 207, 212, 218, 227
Historic Scotland xiii, 56, 151, 216

## I
I Heart UTG 188, 191, 194, 219

## J
Jacobites 15, 17, 19, 23
Jameson, George 3, 5, 8, 129
J F Beattie & Sons *see James Forbes Beattie*

## K
Kennedy, William 19
King Edward VII ix, 71, 99, 110–112, 115, 167, 170–171, 177
King George II 17, 24
King James VI 3

## L
La Torre family 96–97

Links and Parks Committee 30, 163–164, 166, 175
Lord Byron 11, 24–25, 35–36, 118, 120
Lumsden, Louisa 67, 69–70
Lumsden, Robert 9
Lumsden & Robertson, advocates 42, 48, 50, 68, 70–71

## M
Mackenzie, Alexander Marshall xi, 70, 87
Mackintosh, Charles Rennie 170
Mann, Charles 75–76, 90, 165
Mann's Grand see Palace Hotel
Matthews, James xii, 43–45, 47–49, 55, 59, 61, 70, 81, 116–117, 230
Marischal College 11, 17, 21, 56, 68, 71, 76, 78, 99, 129, 131, 164, 229
Millennium Commission 182, 184
Milne Group see Stewart Milne Group
Monkey House 13, 27, 42, 64, 70, 73, 79
Mutton Brae xii, 9, 14, 20–21, 29, 33, 38–39, 41, 43–44, 52, 85, 87, 125, 127–129, 132, 136, 141–142, 207

## N
National Car Parks 177, 179
North Kirk 151–153

## O

## P
Palace Hotel 74–76, 90, 92, 165
Patagonian Court 7, 9, 30, 32, 34, 44, 131
Peacock Visual Arts Centre 184, 187–188, 193, 210, 219
Peacock Group, the 184, 188, 191
Pennant, Thomas 29, 33–34, 36–37
Plantation, the 40–43, 48
Planted Bank, the 40, 48, 54, 65, 68
Playe Green 1–3, 14, 43
Police Committee 50
Prince Albert 58–59, 64, 72, 74, 86, 99–101, 110–111, 115–116, 167
Public Library xii, 77, 87, 90, 122–123, 143, 146, 154, 162
Public Toilets, Gents and Ladies ix, 111, 115, 166–171, 224

## Q
Queen Elizabeth 3
Queen Victoria 40, 59, 72–73, 83, 99–102
Queen's Road 1, 6, 9
Queen Street Church see North Kirk

## R
Referendum 201–205, 220–221, 231

# INDEX

Rettie, James 13, 33
Rising, the 15, 17, 19, 22
Robert Gordon's College xii, 2, 18, 34, 36, 84, 117, 120, 177
Robert Gordon's Hospital 19, 34–36, 46
Robert Gordon's University 119, 227, 231
Robertson & Lumsden *see Lumsden & Robertson*
Rosemount Viaduct viii, ix, xii, 9, 14, 19, 34–35, 63, 77–78, 81–82, 85–87, 89–90, 92, 101–102, 110, 115, 123, 142–144, 162, 166, 177, 208, 211, 213–214, 227
Rose Walk ix, 172–173
Royal Commission on the Ancient and Historic Monuments of Scotland (RCAHMS) ix, 171
Rubislaw Den 1, 57, 61
*Rus in urbe* 60, 63

## S

Salmond, Alex 187
Schoolhill 3, 8, 10, 20–21, 29, 34–35, 37–38, 51, 82, 84, 111, 117, 120–121, 125–126, 132, 153–154, 177, 207–208, 229
Schoolhill handloom factory 21, 38, 41, 125–127, 130, 132, 135
Scottish Enterprise 180, 184, 188, 190, 200, 211, 214, 231

Scottish National Party (SNP) 204, 238
Scottish North Eastern Railway 139
*Scotsman*, the 96, 192
Shakespeare, William 3
Shepherd, Mike ix, xiii, 178, 187, 202–203, 221
Sheep ix, 1, 6, 7, 9, 14, 34, 50, 61, 212, 229
Simpson, Archibald 36, 46, 61, 64, 66–67, 80, 129, 132–134, 146, 147
Sir Alex Ferguson 160, 213
Sir Ian Wood 179, 187–188, 193, 198, 200, 202, 206–209, 216, 219
Skene Road 7
Skene Street 9, 35, 40, 47, 64, 77, 80, 82, 212
Skene Terrace 40, 41, 43–44, 52, 64, 77–78, 92, 95–96
Skene Turnpike 1, 6, 9, 34, 57
Slessor, Mary ix, 136–138
Smith, Henry Bain 108, 110, 119
South Free Church 63, 87, 90, 123–124, 133, 143–144, 162
South United Free Church *see South Free Church*
Spa Well 2, 4, 36, 38
Special Committee on Improvement 47–50, 82, 102
St Elizabeth Kirche 134–135, 147

St Mark's Church *see South Free Church*
St Nicholas Church 2, 5, 19, 44, 66, 132, 144, 148, 162
Stevenson, Grant 101, 108
Stewart Milne Group 151, 153–154
Stuart, Charles Edward 17

**T**

Tax Incremental Financing (TIF) 198, 205–206, 220, 222
Triple Kirks, the ix, xii, 34–35, 39, 44, 51, 63, 82, 85, 87–88, 122–123, 125, 128–129, 131, 133–136, 142–147, 151–155, 182, 208, 230

**U**

Union Bridge 10, 11, 13, 27, 32–33, 39, 43, 46, 52, 61, 64, 85, 89–90, 99, 110, 130, 134, 139–140, 157, 160, 169, 177, 182, 189, 207, 211, 213
Union Street 11–12, 14, 40, 53, 59, 61, 63, 65–66, 70, 75, 110–111, 115, 117, 123, 129–131, 133, 141, 160, 167, 169, 177, 180, 182, 190, 207–208, 210, 214
Union Terrace viii, ix, xi, xii, 13, 30, 33, 40–43, 47–51, 54, 63–68, 70, 72–79, 82, 85, 87, 89–90, 92–95, 99–102, 108, 110–111, 115, 123, 136, 138, 141, 146, 156, 165–167, 178, 184, 207, 212–213, 230
United Presbyterian Church 123, 143
Upperkirkgate 17, 67, 171

**V**

Victoria Park 47, 49, 163, 165–166
Victoria Park Fountain 49, 164–166

**W**

Wallace, William viii, 85, 96, 101, 105, 110, 117, 162
Webs 10, 21, 26, 33, 38–39
Well of Spa *see Spa Well*
West Free Church 63, 123, 133, 142–144, 147, 157
Westerkirkgate 5, 7, 17
Wilson, Robert 77
Windmill Brae 7, 9, 12–13, 66, 141
Wood, Ian *see Sir Ian Wood*
Wooded Bank, the 40, 44, 47–50, 54
Wooded Slopes, the 40, 48
Woodside Works 21, 126–127, 229
Woolmanhill xi, 1–2, 4, 6–7, 9, 14, 19, 21, 25, 34, 36, 38–40, 43, 49, 51, 63, 69, 77, 85, 89, 125, 133, 139, 141, 157–158, 160, 208
Woolmanhill Hospital 44, 64, 154, 161
Wyness, Fenton 3

# BY THE SAME AUTHOR

*Lost Aberdeen*

*Lost Aberdeen: The Outskirts*

*Lost Aberdeen: The Freedom Lands*

*Footdee and her Shipyards*

*Round About Mounthooly*

*The Spital*

*The Spital Lands*

*Old Aberdeen*

*A Monumental Business: The Story of A & J Robertson (Granite) Ltd 1876–2001*

*The Granite Mile*